MARTIN HEIDEGGER

THE QUESTION OF BEING

Translated with an Introduction

by

WILLIAM KLUBACK and JEAN T. WILDE

COLLEGE & UNIVERSITY PRESS · *Publishers*
NEW HAVEN, CONN.

ACKNOWLEDGMENT

We are indebted to Professor William Kimmel of Hunter College, whose encouragement and advice have contributed to whatever value these volumes may have in stimulating a discussion of German philosophy in the United States. We are also indebted to Vittorio Klostermann of Frankfurt, Germany, for the permission to translate the text of Martin Heidegger.

To

MICHAEL WEISS

and

KATE and HANS LANGE

CONTENTS

PREFACE

This volume is the second in a series of translations of the works of Martin Heidegger which attempts to present his philosophy and at the same time critically analyze and discuss the implications of his thought. Philosophy cannot be discussed without history. History is the progressive revelation of the structures of thought. It is the concretization of the *Geist*. In Heidegger the theological and philosophical presuppositions of German Idealism are fulfilled insofar as he has preserved the understanding of the struggle between light and darkness, divine and human, good and evil. His failure to find the ground of their reconciliation points to the fact that while Heidegger is the fulfillment of Idealism he is at the same time its destruction. In the overcoming of Idealism, theology slips away from philosophy, revealing only the possibility of a poetical reconciliation of the human crisis. There are indications in Heidegger's writings that poetry is neither enough nor satisfactory. The haunting demands of the Schelling of 1841-42 for a God, demanded by the will, to whom man can pray and before whom all knees are bent, appear in Heidegger's last work, *Identität und Differenz*.

German Idealism was rooted in the theological teachings of Johann Albrecht Bengel and Friedrich Christoph Oetinger. These two Swabian Pietist theologians disseminated the thought of Jacob Boehme, revealing the fact that the structure of German Idealism flows from Luther. Heidegger, insofar as he reveals the Schelling of Munich and Berlin—a Schelling deeply influenced by Schleiermacher—embodies the poetical and religious visions of a universe hidden by Satan but at the same time revealing the Light (Being). Heidegger is deeply immersed in the Nothing (Satan) as the veiling of Being (Light), in the anxiety, deepened by the shocking realization of demonic possibilities,

lying at the root of earthly reality. Salvation may lie in the poetically lived existence; thus Hölderlin or Hebel become his inspiration.

The nineteenth and twentieth centuries spelled out the Satanic domination of *isms* and thus caused Heidegger to say that pessimism and optimism have become laughable terms. His own demonic honeymoon with the Nazis is only another proof of the proportions which the human alliance with Satan can take. Heidegger is the grave digger of German Idealism which was rooted in the Mediator, in reconciliation, in history, in the Golden Age (Oetinger). Heidegger knows no Mediator but poetry. Heidegger knows no world but the material one in which he attempts to find meaning and reconciliation. In this way Heidegger destroyed the Idealist reconciliation of the spiritual and material worlds as revealing each other, through faith for Bengel or reason for Hegel. Heidegger has no cosmology. Anxiety becomes the basic reality insofar as man, having lost belief in the reconciliation of Idealism, is in a state of anxiety in the face of its rejection. The spiritual (*geistige*) world is lost. This fact reveals the human reality of man "being here" (*Dasein*). The *Dasein* reveals our anxiety.

Heidegger is a crisis philosopher expressing the anxiety of man in a world of new Satanic dimensions which veils Being and points to a life conditioned and revealed by death. In pointing to the anxiety of our age Heidegger uncovered again the Satanic or demonic realities of existence. In his philosophy the Nothingness has led him to the edge of faith. The development of his thought reveals the itinerary of the spirit which goes from rejection toward reconciliation.

A HEIDEGGERIAN LIMITATION

One of the most significant modern attempts to define the meaning of human existence is that of the German philosopher Martin Heidegger. Philosophy for Heidegger is the dialogue between Being and being.[1] The pre-Socratics were philosophers, and here in particular, Heidegger refers to Heraclitus and Parmenides, because their very language revealed the revealing philosophical realities. Language now has departed from its task of revealing and tries only to represent and classify. The poet, Sophocles or Hölderlin, is a revealer of reality because his language captures the Being of being. The poet's language, as in the case of Hölderlin and Sophocles, allows the Being of being to appear and manifest itself. Thus man listens to philosophy because philosophy is concerned with Being and Being is the source and ground of being.

When philosophy with Aristotle and Plato turned from Being to being as the fundamental question of metaphysics, according to Heidegger, they divided and estranged Being from being. This, for Heidegger, was a decisive moment in the history of philosophy. This concern for being was continued in the Middle Ages and dominated modern philosophy to Nietzsche. The Platonic separation of a world of Ideas and a world of opinion opened the gap between Being and being and destroyed the fundamental ontological inseparability of the Being of being. For Heidegger the pre-Socratics represent the most significant historical philosophical period while Plato, Aristotle and Des-

1. *Sein,* Being, is that permanent reality within being (existence) which endures and remains and finally disposes us to the meaning of being (*Seiendes*) or appearance. Thus the necessary distinction between Being (source, ground, and power) with a capital "B" and being (concrete forms of existence) with a small "b."

cartes manifest a decline when we affirm the ontological question of the nature of Being to be the fundamental one. It is in reaction to a philosophy rooted in being that Heidegger begins his re-evaluation and re-direction of European thought.

Philosophy has been predominantly involved in an under-standing of man and Heidegger has attempted to face this prob-lem in an ontological way. His thought, however, shows limita-tions and a serious incompleteness with respect to an adequate philosophical analysis of the meaning of human existence. Hei-degger's limitation lies in the fact that he has failed to consider man within both an ontological and a practical framework. He fails to understand that man's external life expressed in his politi-cal, economic and social experience determines and reveals the ontological nature of his existence. Heidegger in *Sein und Zeit* and *Einführung in die Metaphysik* analyzes the ontological mean-ing of man and shows that man *is* only insofar as his being reveals to him a primal Being through which he becomes conscious of himself existing. In the *Brief über Humanismus* ethical and moral questions are posed but Heidegger, after having analyzed the ontological meaning of man, fails to provide adequately for a moral or ethical framework.

If we accept Heidegger's thesis that the ontological dimension of man points to man's most meaningful aspect because it says that man in his uniqueness reveals the human dimension to him-self, we begin our discussion with two words, "man is." The noun "man" in its relation to the verb "is" reveals its dimension to be an ontological one. The ontological dimension attempts to measure the meaning and uniqueness of man but only in an ontological way. The verb "is" refers to the dimension of the noun "man" and refers to nothing beyond the noun. Implied in the structure of thought is the statement: man is man. Heidegger is concerned with the dimension of man ontologically and main-tains that man becomes conscious of his being as Being insofar as man's being in the world reveals to him something about his dimension and uniqueness. In the religious framework it was man's relation to God or his separation from God which revealed the human dimension. The Heideggerian position thus states

that being has no dimension beyond the ontological. Heidegger's statement about existence is that Man is revealed through man. The ontological is the primal structure of man and, for Heidegger, constitutes the total dimension of man.

To equate man exclusively with his ontological structure is inadequate. The inadequacy of this position lies in the fact that man, ontologically revealed and defined, can be conscious of this state of being only insofar as it realizes itself as being something other than the practical states of being such as the political, social, and economic. These forms are for the ontological, the "other." These "other" forms of being are historical and describe man's doings, creations, and achievements. These are descriptive items or adjectives. They describe man as he does things. These adjectival qualifications belong to man and describe him, not ontologically but historically.

The ontological dimension of man transcends all adjectival qualifications. The adjective can only describe one aspect of the ontological dimension but cannot exhaust it or identify itself with it. The dimension of Being transcends all other dimensions and each adjective can bring forth only one aspect of Being. It is this fact which limits each adjectival qualification and points to the inexhaustible nature of Being.

The adjectives give us this statement: man (in his historical dimension) is political, economic, and social. The "other" of the ontological, the adjective, is necessarily implied in the ontological, because, being the "other," it allows the ontological to measure its dimension as "other" than the adjective. Being "other" than the adjective, it reveals that it is not the adjective nor can be adjective, but at the same time only through the adjective does it know itself to be "other" and itself at the same time. The same reasoning can be applied to the adjective. The adjective can be conscious of its dimension because the "other" is the ontological dimension. The adjective measures itself in relation to its "other" becoming conscious of itself and its "other" at the same time and being conscious of itself as constituting the "other" of the ontological. With this relation we arrive at an understanding which points to the fact that neither the ontological nor the

13

practical in themselves can account for man. A definition of man is possible only when we understand that in a statement such as, "Man is political," both the noun and adjective are seen to reveal the verb, "is." This occurs when the ontological meaning of man measures its dimension in relation to its "other," the adjective which belongs to the ontological dimension by virtue of the fact that this dimension knows itself through the adjective. The same holds for the adjective. If the adjective is considered apart from the noun it could not reveal itself to itself, but the noun being the "other" of the adjective is at the same time the reality through which the adjective limits its own dimensions and reveals itself. To speak of adjective or noun in other but related terms, i.e., implying each other, is to deny the truth that the meaningfulness and significance of each lies not in its own form but its own form comes to a consciousness of itself through its other. The content of each term finds its necessary form in relation to the other. Thus "man" and "political" reveal the verb "is"; neither one alone can accomplish this. Realizing their particular dimensions through each other they state something about the human dimension. The human dimension is neither political nor man; it is both, each possessing individuality, and at the same time the individuality of each achieves its form and dimension through the other. Heidegger's attempts to explain the meaning of man within the ontological dimension can be achieved only if he also attempts to find the relationship between the ontological dimension and the practical dimension. To disregard the practical dimension is to hinder the full realization of the ontological dimension.

The history of philosophical thought gives examples of the philosopher's attempt to reconcile ontology and existence. Plato was one of the first philosophers to be concerned with this reconciliation. The *Protagoras* illustrates Plato's attempt to think in both ontological and practical terms when speaking about man. In the *Protagoras* we are faced with two myths. The first myth describes the creation of the world and man's distinct place in it. This place is characterized by reason which distinguishes man from beast. However, possessed of reason, man cannot survive because without a political and social order reason cannot mani-

fest itself. Man is by nature political and social because apart from a political and social order there is chaos and destruction. Zeus, in the second myth, provided man with political wisdom. Fearing man's self-destruction, Zeus gave all men this political wisdom.

These myths demonstrate the inability of reason apart from its relation to and manifestation in a political and social order, to fulfill man's need. This means that reason can lead to an elucidation of the ontological structure of man and be identified with it but the structure which it reveals is realized in the positing of its "other," the political and social. In this case reason is related to the political and social order and in this relation reason reveals the ontological dimension and at the same time its necessary relationship to the political and social dimensions. Reason realizes its nature as theoretical in terms of the practical and its practical nature in terms of the theoretical. The two myths imply each other insofar as they are the "other" for each other and give each other meaning.

Plato recognized that the dimension of man could be understood only if the theoretical and practical dimensions would relate themselves to each other in such a way as to reveal each other. Man was both practically and ontologically rooted. Neither explanation of man is self-sufficient; both are necessary.

Heidegger has attempted to re-direct thought from an exclusive concern with the adjectival dimension of being to the problem of the ontological dimension of man. He is concerned with the question: What does it mean to be? The ontological analysis, however, can reveal only one aspect of man. Plato's concern with man in the political relationship is the necessary "other" of the ontological dimension. This Heidegger has not shown, and its consequence was his failure to speak as a philosopher against Nazism. He at first accepted Nazism and then withdrew to the "splendid isolation" of the Black Forest. His thought reveals political and ethical emptiness. The ontological uniqueness of man does not prevent the loss of his political, economic, or social freedom. If, however, the economic, political and social dimension takes its limits and gives form to its content through the reali-

zation that the ontological is its "other" then the uniqueness of man, given him ontologically, is realized and preserved in a political, social, and economic life. The legitimacy of the political framework is rooted in the ontological dimension. Neither the ontological dimension nor the political dimension are strange to each other; they are "other" to each other; they reveal each other.

If Heidegger has failed to give an adequate political or ethical philosophy, Marxism, on the other hand, has revealed the danger of a philosophy which disregards the ontological dimension and subsumes man under the economic framework. In this disregard of the ontological, man loses the being "other" to the economic. The economic becomes daemonic. The economic is daemonic, because it is no longer a conditioned reality but becomes an unconditioned reality. Man in the daemonic situation becomes a slave; he is no longer ontologically some-thing. Heidegger has heroically attempted to reestablish man as ontologically some-thing, in face of the Marxist's destruction of the ontological dimension of being. On the other hand, the liberalism of John Stuart Mill, the political wisdom of Thomas Jefferson and Benjamin Franklin, provide the Anglo-Saxon tradition with a body of thought capable of evaluating the place and significance of the state in relation to man. While this tradition is, however, not rooted in the ontological dimension of being but in the "other" of the ontological dimension, that is, the political, it does not fall into the error of identifying the political and ontological dimensions as did Marx. A German philosopher rooted in the ontological dimension might conceivably see the fullness of his thinking achieved in the political and social philosophy of such Anglo-Saxon philosophers as Mill, Jefferson, and Franklin.

The daemonic nature of Marxism and all Totalitarianism points to the fact that a philosophy rooted exclusively in the adjectival dimensions cannot save man from destruction. A genuine ontology reveals how the distortion of the human situation comes about and shows the reality of this daemonic distortion of man. A realization of the daemonic leads to an understanding of Heidegger's attempt to re-discover the ontological dimensions of man. His limitations reveal the insufficiency of the ontological

dimension alone to guarantee the structures of concrete existence against their possible self-destruction. And, on the other hand, he reveals the necessity of the ontological to establish the limits of the adjectival dimensions of being. This need, as we have shown, is rooted in the very structure of Being and flows from it necessarily. The richness of Heidegger's thinking can be fulfilled by its union with the richness of Anglo-American political philosophy. While at present they are estranged from each other, they are not strange to each other and, therefore, rather belong to each other and demand each other. In separation each faces the possibility of daemonic distortion and disintegration.

AN ONTOLOGICAL CONSIDERATION OF "PLACE"

One of the fundamental problems arising from the conflict of state and individual is that of "place." The problem is to understand the relationship between the ontological dimension of being and the political structure of human existence.

The political structure of Europe underwent severe changes during the nineteenth and twentieth centuries.

The powerful edifice of the French monarchy that Louis XVI inherited from his predecessors apparently crumbled to pieces as the result of a train of events set in motion by the unsolved fiscal problems arising from the American wars; the Romanov Empire fell only when millions of lives had been sacrificed; and when it did so, it brought down its two rivals to destruction with it. Upon the ruins of these three Empires there arose in our own day states making still greater demands upon their citizens, and exercising absolutisms more all-embracing than any hitherto known.[1]

In addition to the political changes, but deeply involved in them, was the shocking effect of the loss of religious traditions which had inspired literature and philosophy. Only science was free from the effects of the loss. The religious faiths of Europe had provided the inspiration for the philosophies of Descartes, Leibniz, Spinoza, Kant, Hegel, and Schelling. Utopian socialism, Marxism, Comtianism, statism are only a few of the "isms" involved in the transformation of European society and in the destruction of its traditions. In a startling way the emphasis on history in the nineteenth Century resulted in the loss of the historical consciousness. History could not resist the destruction of

1. Max Beloff, *The Age of Absolutism*, (London, 1954), p. 172.

cosmology, Kantian ethics, or natural law. This change necessitated a new evaluation of the ontological meaning of man. Man was now seen to be rooted in the daemonic distortive possibility of earthly ideals which had been substituted for the religiously inspired thought of previous centuries.

Thus the problem of the relation between ontology and politics has become acute. With new political dimensions, philosophy considers ontological dimensions and attempts to order both in order to reveal an ordering order that relates man to society. This relating relates man, who reveals an already existing relation to society, to a unique ground of existence. It is in a discussion of the ontological meaning of "place" that these two inseparable but estranged relationships in man come forth.

"Place" places man in that dimension which reveals the revealing meaning of Being. Man is involved in "place" in two dimensions, horizontal and vertical. The horizontal dimension is determined by his political relationship. Vertically, being is a dimension hiding the uniqueness of Being, but at the same time it is the place of Being. "Place" places man in such a way that it reveals the external bounds of his existence and at the same time the depths of his freedom and reality. "Place" places the uniqueness of man in that dimension where any adjectival qualification, such as political, social, or economic, is the description of only one aspect of his being, leaving the depths of the vertical dimension untouched and excluded. The vertical dimension of being is the house of Being from which meaning and structure arise and become constitutive of the horizontal dimension. The two dimensions appear in separation but are housed in unity and reveal each other to each other. In thought, communication, and action, whose end is to preserve or to change, the horizontal dimension reflects the ground of Being in so far as the ground proceeds to externalization, externalizing its Nothingness (unrealized possibility) into something. In the processing of the process of Being, its abysmal freedom comes to light. Thought, communication, and action concretize the house of Being and reveal the nothingness which is something, reveal the "place" which is the unique dwelling of being, the thing (dwelling) which is the

gathering of being in Being. The realization realizing dwelling points to the "being here in this world," for only here does man dwell in the house of Being and only here is he conscious of it, and thus of a relation to God as being above him as the heavens are above the earth. Thus the dwelling of man is the consciousness of his mortality and his dwelling on the earth. Man's uniqueness and distinctness, ontologically considered, dialectically determines the structure of his external dwelling. The fact that his being implies his dwelling also points to the fact that his ontological uniqueness transcends his external being and justifies external being in so far as its reality is the realization of the ontological dimension of the human reality. Life, liberty, and the pursuit of happiness are rooted in being in so far as they point to the unveiling of Being. They point to Being because their very dimensions reveal the uniqueness of being. This is why we say they are self-evident and necessarily implied in man. With these concepts the eighteenth century showed an awareness of the constitutive nature of human reality and reflected the traditional understanding of "place" found in the Greeks and in St. Thomas.

Heidegger again attempts a philosophy of "place" but only within an ontological framework. This redefinition of man in relation to place demonstrates Heidegger's positive attempt to rediscover man apart from history, from economic or sociological determinism, and *Weltanschauung*. "Place," however, cannot be redefined unless its tension in and estrangement from the political order is dialectically formulated and understood. The Thomistic conception of natural law must be justified if ontological "place" and freedom are to be preserved and valued. The natural order can not remain strange to the ontological dimension but must reveal it as the source of its own meaning and justification.

The horizontal and vertical dimensions of Being are not strange to each other, but in the history of nineteenth and twentieth century thought after German idealism there developed a radical gap between the "concrete" and the pointing beyond the concrete. *"Man ist, was er isst,"*[2] characterized the perspective of

2. Man is what he eats.

the century. Abstract rights were buried by historicism; *Weltanschauung* and anthropological philosophy became substitutes for ontology. Metaphysics was dead. Being was strange to being and thus the horizontal was strange to the vertical dimension of being.

However, their original unity is rooted in the fact that the ontological and existential dimensions of man posit each other and reveal each other. "Place" is that which is revealed by this revealing relationship of the ontological and political dimensions. Each dimension in itself is an abstract generality which can be conceived but not realized without the other. The comprehension of the being of the ontological and of the political is grounded in their particularization which takes place through each other. The revealing structure of each results from its being grounded in the other and at the same time in a state of difference to the other. Thus "place" comprises both the vertical and the horizontal dimension of being, revealing a state of difference and inseparability. The distortion of this relationship makes the horizontal dimension strange to the vertical and thus unrelated to it. The vertical dimension reveals itself in separation and strangeness to the world, binding satisfaction in aloneness, refusing the world and finally denying it. Thus the world, the mediation between man ontologically and existentially grounded, belongs no longer to him. His existence in the world is an excuse for his employment by another power, the state; he has no "place." The denial of this being is the denial of his vertical dimension; he can no longer reveal the dimensions of his uniqueness in the world, his uniqueness must hide, it lies dormant.

Consciousness of the relation between the ontological and political dimensions is rooted in the experience of man. This relation, however, points to the house of the relation, it places the "place" of man at the point where the external realization of the internal ground separates to form the concrete existential reality as distinguished from its ontological ground. His existence points to this dwelling at every turn. Not only has it pointed to this relationship but it has pointed to the destructive consequences of their separability. To illustrate this fact we turn to the thirteenth

century. The relation between king and baron in feudalism illustrates the concern of man for preservation of "place." Through the acquisition of land man receives rights but also owes rights. Land becomes an essential condition of his place; it becomes the *sine qua non* of the dwelling in which he is conscious of his dimensions both vertically and horizontally. Vertically, it is the place which permits him to reveal the justification of his existence. On the other hand, it is place which relates him to others, his king and fellow barons. His place is inviolable in so far as he has not violated without just cause the place of others. If his place is violated, he has the right of revolt or *diffidatio*.

In England, during the reign of Henry III the Chronicler, Roger of Wendover, tells the following story concerning a struggle between Richard, the Marshal, and Henry III. Henry was dominated by advisers from Poitou who desired to turn him into an absolute monarch violating the traditions of English feudalism in the first half of the 13th Century.

Roger of Wendover gives a very clear insight into the thinking of the Marshal with regard to *diffidatio*, when he describes in detail the answers that the Marshal gave to the demands of the king for his submission. "As to it being my duty, because I have invaded the king's territory, this is not true, for although I was always ready to abide by the law and the decisions of my peers in his court, and often asked the king by messengers to grant me this, he always refused it to me, and himself invaded my territory and attacked me contrary to all the laws of justice. And hoping to please the king by my submission, I freely entered into terms of peace with him, which were very injurious to myself. It was agreed that, unless those terms were observed on the part of the king toward me, I should remain entirely in the same condition as I was before the said peace was agreed on, namely, that I should be free from all homage to him, and in a state of defiance toward him as I had formerly been by action of the Bishop of St. David. As the king had not returned the castle, the state of *diffidatio* was re-established. As Henry failed to observe the peace, I was justified according to my agreement in endeavoring to recover what belonged to me, and in weakening his power by

every means possible, especially as he eagerly sought my destruction. What is more, after the truce of fifteen days, he without a trial deprived me of my office of marshal, which belonged to me and which I hold by hereditary right; nor would he restore it to me when I asked him, therefore, I am not his subject but am released from all fealty to him. . . . Thus I have been justified and am still justified in defending myself, and in thwarting the malicious designs of his advisers by every means in my power.

"It is true that the king is richer and more powerful than I, but he is not more powerful than God, who is all justice, and in whom I place my hopes of safety and of obtaining my rights in the kingdom, and I do not put my trust in foreigners nor do I seek their alliance or assistance. And I well know that the king can bring seven men to my one . . . and I have heard from credible people that the Bishop of Winchester has engaged to bring all England under his control."

Furthermore, the king had accused the Marshal of having attacked the suzerain personally during the battle at Grosmunt in Wales, where the king had entered the Marshal's land. This argument was answered by the Marshal: "as far as it regarded the king personally, it was false; and if any of my retainers had by chance been present there, they only attacked the king's attendants and not the royal person. If they did so, it was not to be wondered at, when the king came into my territory with his army to attack me and injure me in every way. This is plainly proved by letters in which he summoned all throughout England to assist in destroying me.

"And it would not be to the credit of the king if I were to yield to his pleasure when he is not supported by reason, I should rather be offering an insult to him and to justice, which is a king's duty to exercise and to observe toward his subjects. And I should set a bad example to everyone, namely, that of abandoning the cause of justice and the prosecution of my rights on account of an error·in judgment, contrary to all justice, and to the injury of his subjects; for in such a case it would seem that we loved our worldly possessions more than justice."

The story of the Marshal, apart from its bearing on the consti-

tutional history of England, shows that man is a dweller on this earth in a very distinctive way. In the first place to dwell is to be, dwelling thus revealing Being. The Marshal was conscious of his right as dweller in relation to his king, and, because he dwelled, his dwelling established rights and obligations. These rights and obligations not only fixed his uniqueness but related it to society. Thus society was a fabric woven from relations recognized as having their source in individuality and proceeding from individuality to community. Dwelling points to itself and beyond itself. The Marshal acts on the basis of rights not arbitrarily invented but rooted in the fact that in dwelling here on this land is to enter into rights and obligations. His being there is the concretizing of rights inherent in the "being there" already. The "being there" can not be created for its creation would be daemonic. The *ordo ordinatus* destroys the meaning of "place," thus resting in the assumption that "place" is created and can be created by man. Man is a tool of a man-creator. This is the result of the separation of *ordo* from *ordinans,* the separation of being from Being. This separation has shocked the nineteenth and twentieth centuries.

History is the chronicle of man's concern for "place." Man has turned to history in the form of tradition to speak of his rights in relation to the state. Rights, however, mean little if separated from place. Rights can become more or less, they can be differently interpreted, they can be taken away. Rights are generalities existing weakly or strongly depending upon the momentary condition of a particular state and its internal hierarchy of power. War or peace, mobilization or disarmament, prosperity or depression are a few of the conditions determining the confirmation of rights. Can rights be rooted in a more fundamental ground? "Place" places man in the ground of self-consciousness, it confirms him in this world in a unique way. "Place" reveals our being here, our human reality. The attempt to be God is a destruction and distortion of our being; to be an animal is a similar distortion of being; it reveals the perversion of our being and its possibility is our tragedy. These reveal the daemonic possibility of being.

The State dominates our horizontal dimension, it limits our place existentially and it tragically involves us in the destruction of the "place" of others. The very nature of our existence implies at times the destruction of others, both of men and beasts. Nevertheless, our horizontal "place" can never be totally eliminated without the consequent denial of our ontological "place." This is true because ontological place reveals itself through existential "place." If there is no longer existential "place," (if man becomes a mere agent of the state) the vertical dimension of being is entirely destroyed. To be man is to have an existential "place" but this "place" must become the house of our Being in which our ontological dimension, our being here, unfolds and finds fulfillment. "Place" places us both horizontally and vertically; it is the dimension of our ontological and existential uniqueness.

In the horizontal dimension of Being the struggle of existence involves man in the destruction and violation of the "place" of others. Here man tends to destroy man both vertically and horizontally. The realm of political activity becomes the arena in which the tendencies to distort "place" are manifested. The distortion of "place" is daemonic; man becomes beast or attempts to be God. Both dimensions, the beastly and the divine, distort the human dimension and lead to its destruction. The human dimension receives its uniqueness insofar as it reveals the revealing ground of that being who is neither God nor beast, but who is conscious that he is being a being in this world. Thus, a full understanding of "place" reveals the tragedy involved in the loss of "place" and the inclination in man to distort "place."

The tensions of the human situation are manifested in the fact that man is in the vertical and horizontal dimensions of "place," in both empirical and ontological dimensions, and is at the same time estranged from these dimensions. The possibility of estrangement from the ontological dimension in consciousness is the realization of it. To be estranged from "place" is to be at the same time conscious of the placing character of "place." Estrangement from "place" is the shock of the absence of freedom. Estrangement from the empirical dimension results when man is considered an instrument or an employable tool of a social, economic, or

political power. This results in a hiding of the vertical dimension and the consequent destruction of the meaning of "place." The meaning of "place" proceeds from two dimensions, the vertical and horizontal. Each dimension is rooted in the other and reveals its limitations through the other. The limits of the horizontal dimension are grounded in the unrestricted unfolding of the vertical dimension whose freedom is manifested in thought, communication, and action. The right of the horizontal dimension is revealed in its necessity for the housing of the vertical. Insofar as the vertical dimension is permitted to reveal itself, it both guarantees the claims of the horizontal and reveals their limits. A political order is limited in its activities to the preservation of the ontological nature of "place." The disregard of the ontological nature of "place" is the obliteration of human freedom. To have "place" is to be free. To have "place" ontologically and empirically is to have a house in which being can unfold and manifest its Being. Ontological "place" thus precedes the political, social, or economic aspects of existence whose reality lies only in their being adjectival qualifications of Being. They can be protective structures for that freedom which is the ground of ontological "place." Ontological "place" thus defines man before he enters existence, and delineates that being which enters the existential realm and establishes the structures identifiable with the existential realm. "Place" reveals the uniqueness of man and conditions his existential activity. "Place" points both to its unique dimension of Being and to the distortion and perversion which arise from its concealment. "Place" is the house of Being, the revelation of the freedom of man and of the ground of his Being.

FREEDOM AND POWER

The ontological analysis of the human reality demands not only a consideration of freedom but also of power. Power and freedom are ontological dimensions. Power is manifested in the state while freedom is the realization of the uniqueness of man. Man is involved in and introduced to both freedom and power. He is inseparable from the state insofar as he is a political being but separable in the creativity of his individuality.

The relation of freedom, non-being, and anxiety define the uniqueness of man. Consciousness is the realization not only of his uniqueness in freedom but also in power. The creative encounter with life reveals the depths of subjectivity; the state is the concretization of power and the arena of communal involvement. Power is revealed as the structuring order of a totality, the state. The state is not merely the sum of its individual beings, but, being the concretization of power, it has a distinct being of its own. The distinctness of this being is characterized by its law of behavior, which we call *raison d'état*. Its behavior is not that of the individual or of the totality of its individuals. Its morality, at times, contradicts individual morality. Nevertheless, the policy of state is conditioned by the religious, political, and social traditions of its members.

The human reality conceived in terms of individual ontological freedom fails to explain man's involvement in the state. To belong to the state means to be within the structure of power. The state is the house of man in which he is lifted from his exclusive individuality into a higher totality, from which he receives meaning and to whose end he is inseparably related. Existentialism, however, particularly that of Martin Heidegger, seems to have given little consideration to the problem of state and power. If power is as ontological and revelatory of the human reality as is free-

dom, it would appear that an analysis of freedom alone fails to reveal the whole of the human condition. The state is the concretization of power; the collectivity which forms the state permits the state to reveal itself as power. Thus, the collectivity forming the state reveals it to be the instrument of power. *Raison d'état* is the activity of the state attempting to carry out the demands of power. The demands of power realized in the state are not necessarily those of the individual but the expressed will of a totality independent of the individual and yet brought into being by the existence of the individual. This occurs because the new totality is the manifestation of power and not that of the individual will. In the state the individual is ontologically free but also ontologically determined by the power structure of the state. Individuality is inseparably related to its belonging to the state. This belonging is not determined by man's freedom but is the necessary condition of that freedom and revelatory of it. To be is to belong, to be in the state, in the structure of power.

The consciousness of man is posited in his encounter with freedom and the state. It is an encounter with the ontological dialectic of freedom and power. Man defined as a rational being, is the dialectical center of freedom and power. They are revealed to him in their relation to each other. Man, posited in in freedom and power, becomes the conscious center of their relationship. Man is aware of power in the state; he is conscious of its distortive and destructive possibility. Man is conscious of his freedom, its creativeness, and the history of this creativeness; he is conscious of the individuality of his freedom and its unique experiential nature. Not only does man realize the distortive and destructive possibility of power in the state, but he is involved in the same distortive and destructive possibility within himself. Man is the destructive possibility of his own creativeness. Man is therefore, the tragic center as well as the dialectical center of Being. Man can be destroyed by his own creation—which is at once more than its creator—the state; and the distorting possibility of individual creativeness, can destroy man, the

source of creativity. Being both a tragic and dialectical center, man experiences both theoretical and existential estrangement.

German thinkers have analyzed both problems, freedom and power. Martin Heidegger has attempted to explain ontological freedom.[1] Friedrich Meinecke[2] and Gerhard Ritter[3] have analyzed the nature of power and *raison d'état*. Heidegger speaks of neither the state nor power. It would appear that the historians, von Ranke, Treitschke, Burckhardt, Meinecke and Ritter are not known to the existentialist philosopher, Heidegger. To avoid a discussion of power and the state is to have moved to an extreme anti-Hegelian position. If Hegel lost individuality in terms of its concrete existence, Heidegger has lost collective existence in failing to consider political life and the ontological nature of power. Neither power nor freedom alone, ontologically considered, point to the Being of the human reality. Power and freedom together do. Hegel found man's freedom to be posited in consciousness: in the dialectical (rational) reconciliation of the ontological structures of freedom and power.

Heidegger is the philosopher of the *Dasein* (existence). He is concerned with what it means "to be in the world," not only as mind but as concrete being. "Being in the world" reveals the human reality. To be in the world is to be conscious of anxiety and of having to die. Anxiety and death reveal the revealing condition of man. Heidegger attempts to point to this real in the human reality, a reality whose Being reveals itself as "being here." Hegel finds the real of reality in reason, and insofar as reality is real, it is reasonable.

Hegel necessitated Heideggerian existentialism by his conclusion that existence is reconciled in consciousness. (Consciousness equals thought.) For him freedom and power are ontological dimensions of Being. They are grasped by thought and

1. Heidegger, Martin, *Sein und Zeit* (Tübingen, 1953).

2. Meinecke, Friedrich, *Die Idee der Staatsräson* (München and Berlin, 1924).

3. Ritter, Gerhard, *Die Dämonie der Macht* (München, 1948.)

clarified by it. For Heidegger, on the other hand, man is existentially involved in freedom and power, and participates tragically in them. (Consciousness equals *Angst*.) But man is both their dialectical and their tragic center. Dialectically he is involved in them in thought but tragically he is involved in their existential concreteness.

BIBLIOGRAPHY

Secondary Sources

BOCHENSKI, I. M. Contemporary European Philosophy. University of California Press, Berkeley and Los Angeles, 1956, pp. 161-172.

BROCK, W. (Edited by). Existence and Being. Henry Regnery, Chicago, 1949.

BUBER, MARTIN. Between Man and Man, Tr. Ronald Gregor Smith. Routledge and Kegan Paul, London, 1947.

COLLINS, JAMES. The Existentialists. Henry Regnery, Chicago, 1952.

GLICKSMAN, MARJORIE. "A Note on the Philosophy of Heidegger." *Journal of Philosophy*, Vol. 35, No. 4, 1938.

HEINEMANN, F. H. Existentialism and the Modern Predicament. Harper Torchbooks, New York, 1958.

KAUFMANN, WALTER. Existentialism from Dostoevsky to Sartre. Meridian Books, New York, 1956, pp. 33-40, 206-221.

KUHN, HELMUTH. Encounter with Nothingness: An Essay on Existentialism. Henry Regnery, Chicago, 1949.

LÖWITH, KARL. "Heidegger: Problem and Background of Existentialism." *Social Research*, Vol. 15, pp. 345-369.

RUGGIERO, GUIDO. Existentialism: Disintegration of Man's Soul. Social Science Publishers, New York, 1948, pp. 61-67.

SONNEMANN, ULRICH. Existence and Therapy: An Introduction to Phenomenological Psychology and Existential Analysis. Grune and Stratton, New York, 1954.

USSHER, ARLAND. Journey Through Dread. Devin-Adair, New York, 1955, pp. 59-92.

WAHL, JEAN. A Short History of Existentialism. Philosophical Library, New York, 1949.

WILD, JOHN. The Challenge of Existentialism. Indiana University Press, Bloomington, 1955.

WYSCHOGROD, MICHAEL. Kierkegaard and Heidegger: The Ontology of Existence. Routledge and Kegan Paul, London, 1954.

VORWORT

Die Schrift gibt den unveränderten, um einige Zeilen (S. 24 f.) erweiterten Text des Beitrags zur Festschrift für Ernst Jünger (1955). Geändert ist der Titel. Er lautete: *Über »Die Linie«*. Der neue Titel soll anzeigen, daß die Besinnung auf das Wesen des Nihilismus aus einer Erörterung des Seins als ~~Sein~~ herstammt. Nach der Überlieferung versteht die Philosophie unter der Seinsfrage die Frage nach dem Seienden als Seienden. Sie ist *die* Frage der Metaphysik. Die Beantwortung dieser Frage beruft sich jeweils auf eine Auslegung des Seins, die im Fraglosen verbleibt und den Grund und Boden für die Metaphysik bereitstellt. Die Metaphysik geht nicht in ihren Grund zurück. Diesen Rückgang erläutert die »Einleitung« zu »Was ist Metaphysik?«, die seit der 5. Auflage (1949) dem Text des Vortrags vorangestellt ist. (7. Auflage 1955, S. 7—23)

THE QUESTION OF BEING

FOREWORD

This article repeats, unchanged and expanded by a few lines (p. 24f.), the text of the contribution to the publication issued in honor of Ernst Jünger (1955).[1] The title has been changed. It read: *Concerning "The Line."* The new title is meant to indicate that the consideration of the essence of nihilism stems from a discussion of Being as ~~Being~~. According to tradition, the question of being is understood by philosophy to be of being as being. It is *the* question of metaphysics. The answering of this question is always related to an interpretation of Being which remains as yet unquestioned and prepares the ground and basis for metaphysics. Metaphysics does not go back to its ground. This return is explained in the Introduction to *What Is Metaphysics* which has been added to the text of the lecture from the fifth edition (1949) on. (7th edition 1955, pp. 7-23).

---

[1] Ernst Jünger (1895—). His book, *Der Arbeiter. Herrschaft und Gestalt* (1932), is significant for Existentialism since he represents the worker as the exponent of technology and as the prototype of the man who is to be its future victim. *Über die Linie* deals with the consequential nihilism which results from this daemonic technological domination.

ÜBER »DIE LINIE«

Lieber Herr Jünger!

Mein Gruß zu Ihrem sechzigsten Geburtstag übernimmt mit einer geringen Veränderung den Titel der Abhandlung, die Sie bei der gleichen Gelegenheit mir widmeten. Ihr Beitrag »Über die Linie« erschien unterdessen, an einigen Stellen erweitert, als gesonderte Schrift. Sie ist eine »Lagebeurteilung«, die dem »Überqueren« der Linie gilt, erschöpft sich indes nicht im Beschreiben der Lage. Die Linie heißt auch der »Nullmeridian« (S. 29). Sie sprechen (S. 22 und 31) vom »Nullpunkt«. Die Null deutet auf das Nichts und zwar auf das leere. Wo alles dem Nichts zudrängt, herrscht der Nihilismus. Am Nullmeridian nähert er sich seiner Vollendung. Eine Auslegung Nietzsches aufnehmend, verstehen Sie den Nihilismus als den Vorgang, »*daß die obersten Werte sich entwerten*« (Wille zur Macht, Nr. 2, aus dem Jahre 1887).

Die Null-Linie hat als Meridian ihre Zone. Der Bezirk des vollendeten Nihilismus bildet die Grenze zwischen zwei Weltaltern. Die ihn bezeichnende Linie ist die kritische Linie. An ihr entscheidet sich, ob die Bewegung des Nihilismus im nichtigen Nichts verendet oder ob sie der Übergang in den Bereich einer »neuen Zuwendung des Seins« ist (S. 32). Die Bewegung des Nihilismus muß demnach von sich her auf unterschiedene Möglichkeiten angelegt und ihrem Wesen gemäß mehrdeutig sein.

Ihre Lagebeurteilung geht den Zeichen nach, die erkennen lassen, ob und inwiefern wir die Linie überqueren und dadurch aus der Zone des vollendeten Nihilismus heraustreten. Im Titel Ihrer Schrift »Über die Linie« bedeutet das »über« soviel wie: hinüber, trans, μετά. Dagegen verstehen die folgenden Bemer-

34

Concerning "The Line."

Dear Mr. Jünger,

My greetings on the occasion of your sixtieth birthday adopts, with a slight change, the title of the treatise which you dedicated to me on a similar occasion. Your contribution, *Across the Line,* appeared in the meanwhile, enlarged in a few places, as a separate article. It is a "situation appraisal" which refers to the "crossing over" of the line, but is not confined to a description of the situation. The line is also called the "zero meridian" (p. 29). You speak (pp. 22 and 31) of a "zero point." The zero refers to nothingness and, in fact, to empty nothingness. Where everything pushes towards nothingness, nihilism reigns. At the zero meridian it approaches its completion. Taking up an interpretation of Nietzsche, you understand nihilism as the process whereby "the highest values become devaluated" (*Will to Power,* No. 2, from the year 1887).

The zero line has its zone as a meridian. The area of complete nihilism forms the boundary between two eras. The line designating it is the critical line. By means of it is determined whether the movement of nihilism ends in negative nothingness or whether it is the transition to the realm of a "new turning-towards on the part of Being" (p. 32). The movement of nihilism must accordingly be intended of itself for diverse possibilities and, according to its essence, have a number of meanings.

Your estimation of the situation follows the signs which indicate whether and to what extent we cross over the line and thereby step out of the zone of complete nihilism. In the title of your essay *Across the Line,* the *"über"* signifies across, *trans, meta.* However, the following remarks interpret the *"über"* only

35

kungen das »über« nur in der Bedeutung des: de, περί. Sie handeln »von« der Linie selbst, von der Zone des sich vollendenden Nihilismus. Wenn wir beim Bild der Linie bleiben, dann finden wir, daß sie in einem Raum verläuft, der selbst von einem Ort bestimmt wird. Der Ort versammelt. Die Versammlung birgt das Versammelte in sein Wesen. Aus dem Ort der Linie ergibt sich die Herkunft des Wesens des Nihilismus und seiner Vollendung.

Mein Brief möchte an diesen Ort der Linie vordenken und so die Linie erörtern. Ihre Lagebeurteilung unter dem Namen trans lineam und meine Erörterung unter dem Namen de linea gehören zusammen. Jene schließt diese ein. Diese bleibt auf jene angewiesen. Damit sage ich Ihnen nichts Besonderes. Sie wissen, daß eine Beurteilung der Lage des Menschen in Bezug auf die Bewegung des Nihilismus und innerhalb dieser eine zureichende Wesensbestimmung verlangt. Solches Wissen fehlt vielerorts. Der Mangel trübt den Blick bei der Beurteilung unserer Lage. Er macht das Urteil über den Nihilismus leichtfertig und das Auge blind für die Gegenwart »dieses unheimlichsten aller Gäste« (Nietzsche, Wille zur Macht. Zum Plan, WW XV, S. 141). Er heißt der »unheimlichste«, weil er als der unbedingte Wille zum Willen die Heimatlosigkeit als solche will. Darum hilft es nichts, ihm die Tür zu weisen, weil er überall schon längst und unsichtbar im Haus umgeht. Es gilt, diesen Gast zu erblicken und zu durchschauen. Sie schreiben selbst (S. 11): »Eine gute Definition des Nihilismus würde der Sichtbar-Machung des Krebserregers zu vergleichen sein. Sie würde nicht die Heilung bedeuten, wohl aber ihre Voraussetzung, soweit Menschen überhaupt daran mitwirken. Es handelt sich ja um einen Vorgang, der die Geschichte weit übergreift.«

»Eine gute Definition des Nihilismus« könnte man somit von einer Erörterung de linea erwarten, wenn anders das menschenmögliche Bemühen um die Heilung sich einem Geleit trans lineam vergleichen läßt. Zwar betonen Sie, der Nihilismus sei nicht der Krankheit, sowenig wie dem Chaos und dem Bösen gleichzusetzen. Der Nihilismus selbst ist sowenig wie der Krebserreger etwas Krankhaftes. Bezüglich des *Wesens* des Nihilismus gibt es keine Aussicht und keinen sinnvollen An-

in the meaning of *de, peri*. They treat "of" the line itself, of the zone of self-completing nihilism. If we stick to the picture of the line, then we find that it blends in a space which is itself determined by a place. The place assembles. The assemblage, in its essence, contains what is assembled. Out of the place of the line originates the origin of the essence of nihilism and its fulfillment.

My letter would like to think ahead to this place of the line and in that way explain the line. Your estimation under the name of *trans lineam* and my discussion under the name of *de linea* belong together. The former includes the latter. The latter remains dependent on the former. By saying this, I am not telling you anything special. You know that an estimation of the situation of man in respect to the movement of nihilism and within it demands an adequate determination of essence. Such knowledge is lacking in many places. This lack clouds the view in estimating our situation. It makes the judgment of nihilism superficial and the eye blind to the presence "of this strangest [the word *unheimlich* here signifies not having a home] of all guests" (Nietzsche, *Will to Power, The Plan*, WW XV, p. 141). It is called the "strangest" because as the unconditional will to will, it wants homelessness as such. Therefore, it does not help to show it the door because it has long since and invisibly been moving around in the house. The important thing is to get a glimpse of this guest and to see through it. You write (p. 11): "A good definition of nihilism would be comparable to making the cancer bacillus visible. It would not signify a cure but perhaps the presupposition of it, insofar as men contribute anything towards it. It involves an event which goes far beyond history."

"A good definition of nihilism" might thus be expected of a discussion *de linea* provided that the effort within the power of man to effect a cure can be compared to being escorted *trans lineam*. To be sure you emphasize that nihilism is not to be placed on an equal basis with sickness, or just as little, on a basis with chaos and evil. Nihilism itself, as little as is the cancer bacillus, is something diseased. In regard to the *essence* of nihilism there is no prospect and no meaningful claim to a cure.

spruch auf Heilung. Gleichwohl bleibt die Haltung Ihrer Schrift eine ärztliche, was schon die Gliederung in Prognose, Diagnose, Therapie andeutet. Der junge Nietzsche nennt den Philosophen einmal den »Arzt der Kultur« (WW X, S. 225). Aber jetzt handelt es sich nicht mehr nur um die Kultur. Sie sagen mit Recht: »Das Ganze steht auf dem Spiel«. »Es geht um den Planeten überhaupt« (S. 28). Das Heilen kann sich nur auf die bösartigen Folgen und bedrohlichen Begleiterscheinungen dieses planetarischen Vorganges beziehen. Um so dringlicher benötigen wir die Kenntnis und Erkenntnis des Erregers, d. h. des Wesens des Nihilismus. Um so nötiger wird das Denken, gesetzt, daß sich eine zureichende Erfahrung des Wesens nur im entsprechenden Denken vorbereitet. Doch im gleichen Maße wie die Möglichkeiten für eine unmittelbar wirksame Heilung schwinden, hat sich auch schon das Vermögen des Denkens verringert. Das Wesen des Nihilismus ist weder heilbar noch unheilbar. Es ist das Heil-lose, als dieses jedoch eine einzigartige Verweisung ins Heile. Soll sich das Denken dem Bereich des Wesens des Nihilismus nähern, dann wird es notwendig vorläufiger und dadurch anders.

Ob eine Erörterung der Linie »eine gute Definition des Nihilismus« beibringen kann, ob sie dergleichen auch nur anstreben darf, wird einem vorläufigen Denken fragwürdig. Eine Erörterung der Linie muß anderes versuchen. Der hierdurch ausgesprochene Verzicht auf eine Definition scheint die Strenge des Denkens preiszugeben. Es könnte aber auch geschehen, daß jener Verzicht das Denken erst auf den Weg einer Anstrengung bringt, die erfahren läßt, welcher Art die sachgerechte Strenge des Denkens ist. Dies läßt sich niemals vom Richterstuhl der Ratio herab entscheiden. Sie ist durchaus kein gerechter Richter. Sie stößt unbedenklich alles *ihr* Ungemäße in den vermeintlichen und überdies von ihr selbst ausgegrenzten Sumpf des Irrationalen. Die Vernunft und ihr Vorstellen sind nur *eine* Art des Denkens und keineswegs durch sich selbst bestimmt, sondern durch jenes, was das Denken geheißen hat, in der Weise der Ratio zu denken. Daß sich deren Herrschaft als Rationalisierung aller Ordnungen, als Normung, als Nivellierung im Zuge der Entfaltung des europäischen Nihilismus

Nevertheless, the attitude of your essay is a medical one, as is already indicated by its organization into prognosis, diagnosis, therapy. The young Nietzsche once called the philosopher the "physician of civilization" (WW X, p. 225). But now it is no longer a question only of civilization. You say quite rightly: "The whole is at stake." "The entire planet is at stake" (p. 28). Healing can only bear upon the malignant results and dangerous symptoms of this planetary event. Even more urgently we need knowledge and recognition of the bacillus, that is, of the essence of nihilism. Even more necessary is thought, assuming that an adequate experience of the essence is provided by suitable thinking. However, to the same degree as the possibilities of an immediately effective healing are disappearing, the ability of thinking has also already lessened. The essence of nihilism is neither healable nor unhealable. It is the heal-less, but as such a unique relegation into health. If thinking is to approach the domain of the essence of nihilism, then it necessarily becomes more temporary and thereby different.

Whether a discussion of the line can bring about "a good definition of nihilism," whether it may even strive for anything of the sort, becomes doubtful to precursory thinking. A discussion of the line must attempt something else. The rejection of a definition expressed hereby seems to sacrifice the strictness of thinking. It might also happen, however, that such a rejection first brings thinking in the direction of an effort which makes it possible to find out the nature of the pertinent strictness of thinking. This can never be decided from the judgment seat of the *ratio*. The latter is by no means a just judge. It unscrupulously pushes everything not in conformity with *it* into the presumable swamp of the irrational, which it itself has staked out. Reason and its conceptions are only *one* kind of thinking and are by no means determined by themselves but by that which has been called thinking, to think in the manner of the *ratio*. That its dominance arises as rationalization of all categories, as establishing norms, as leveling in the course of the unfolding of European nihilism,

aufrichtet, gibt ebenso zu denken wie die dazugehörenden Fluchtversuche in das Irrationale.

Am bedenklichsten ist jedoch der Vorgang, daß sich der Rationalismus und der Irrationalismus gleichermaßen in ein Wechselgeschäft verstricken, aus dem sie nicht nur nicht heraus finden, sondern nicht mehr heraus wollen. Man leugnet darum jede Möglichkeit ab, nach der das Denken vor ein Geheiß gelangen könnte, das sich außerhalb des Entweder-Oder von rational und irrational hält. Ein solches Denken könnte indes durch das vorbereitet werden, was in den Weisen der geschichtlichen Erläuterung, der Besinnung und der Erörterung tastende Schritte versucht.

Der von Ihnen dargelegten ärztlichen Lagebeurteilung möchte meine Erörterung begegnen. Sie schauen und gehen über die Linie hinüber; ich blicke erst nur auf die von Ihnen vorgestellte Linie. Eines verhilft dem anderen wechselweise in die Weite und Klarheit des Erfahrens. Beides könnte helfen, die »hinreichende Kraft des Geistes« (S. 28) zu wecken, die für ein Überqueren der Linie in den Anspruch genommen ist.

Damit wir den Nihilismus in der Phase seiner Vollendung erblicken, müssen wir seine Bewegung in ihrer Aktion durchgehen. Die Beschreibung dieser Aktion ist dann besonders einprägsam, wenn sie als Beschreibung selber an der Aktion teilnimmt. Die Beschreibung gerät dadurch aber auch in eine außerordentliche Gefahr und vor eine weit hinauslangende Verantwortung. Wer in solcher Weise beteiligt bleibt, dessen Verantwortung muß sich in derjenigen Ant-wort versammeln, die aus einem unentwegten Fragen innerhalb der größtmöglichen Fragwürdigkeit des Nihilismus entspringt und als die Ent-sprechung zu dieser übernommen und ausgetragen wird.

Ihr Werk »Der Arbeiter« (1932) hat die Beschreibung des europäischen Nihilismus in seiner Phase nach dem ersten Weltkrieg geleistet. Es entfaltet sich aus Ihrer Abhandlung »Die Totale Mobilmachung« (1930). »Der Arbeiter« gehört in die Phase des »aktiven Nihilismus« (Nietzsche). Die Aktion des Werkes bestand – und besteht in gewandelter Funktion noch – darin, daß es den »totalen Arbeitscharakter« alles Wirklichen aus der Gestalt des Arbeiters sichtbar macht. So erscheint der

provides food for thought, just as do the concomitant attempts at flight into irrational.

What is most serious, however, is that rationalism and irrationalism are entangled in a sort of reciprocal intercourse out of which they not only cannot find their way, but no longer wish to extricate themselves. Therefore, every possibility is denied by which thinking might face a demand which is outside of the either/or of the rational and irrational. Such thinking could, however, be prepared for by what is taking faltering steps in the ways of historical elucidation, reflection, and explanation.

My explanation would like to meet halfway the medical diagnosis of the situation you present. You look and cross over the line; I look first only at the line you present. One reciprocally assists the other in the breadth and clarity of experience. Both could help to arouse the "adequate strength of the mind" (p. 28) which is required for a crossing of the line.

In order that we may see nihilism in the phase of its completion we must accompany its movement in action. The description of this action is especially impressive when, as a description, it itself participates in the action. However, the description thereby runs into extreme danger and faces a far-reaching responsibility. The responsibility of whoever participates in such a manner must be collected in that response which arises from an unswerving questioning within the greatest possible ability of questioning nihilism and be adopted and carried out as corresponding to the latter.

Your essay, *The Worker* (1932) has achieved a description of European nihilism in its phase after World War I. It develops out of your treatise *Total Mobilization* (1930). *The Worker* belongs in the phase of "active nihilism" (Nietzsche). The action of the work consisted—and in a changed function still consists—in the fact that it makes the "total work character" of all reality visible from the figure of the worker. Thus nihilism, which at

anfänglich nur europäische Nihilismus in seiner planetarischen Tendenz. Indessen gibt es keine Beschreibung an sich, die es vermöchte, das Wirkliche an sich zu zeigen. Jede Beschreibung bewegt sich, je schärfer sie vorgeht, umso entschiedener auf ihre besondere Art in einem bestimmten Gesichtskreis. Sehweise und Gesichtskreis – Sie sagen »Optik« – ergeben sich dem menschlichen Vorstellen aus Grunderfahrungen des Seienden im Ganzen. Ihnen geht aber schon eine vom Menschen nie erst machbare Lichtung dessen vorauf, wie das Seiende »ist«. Die Grunderfahrung, die Ihr Vorstellen und Darstellen trägt und durchzieht, erwuchs in den Materialschlachten des ersten Weltkrieges. Das Seiende im Ganzen aber zeigt sich Ihnen im Lichte und im Schatten der Metaphysik des Willens zur Macht, die Nietzsche in der Form einer Wertlehre auslegt.

Im Winter 1939 auf 1940 erläuterte ich in einem kleinen Kreis von Universitätslehrern den »Arbeiter«. Man staunte, daß ein so hellsichtiges Buch seit Jahren vorlag und man selber noch nicht gelernt hatte, einmal den Versuch zu wagen, den Blick auf die Gegenwart in der Optik des »Arbeiters« sich bewegen zu lassen und planetarisch zu denken. Man spürte, daß hiefür auch die universalhistorische Betrachtung der Weltgeschichte nicht zureiche. Man las damals eifrig die »Marmorklippen«, aber, wie mir schien, ohne den hinreichend weiten, d. h. planetarischen Horizont. Man war aber auch nicht überrascht, daß ein Versuch, den »Arbeiter« zu erläutern, überwacht und schließlich unterbunden wurde. Denn es gehört zum Wesen des Willens zur Macht, das Wirkliche, das er be-mächtigt, nicht in *der* Wirklichkeit erscheinen zu lassen, als welche er selber west.

Sie erlauben mir, daß ich eine Aufzeichnung aus dem genannten Erläuterungsversuch wiedergebe. Es geschieht deshalb, weil ich hoffe, in diesem Brief einiges deutlicher und freier sagen zu können. Die Notiz lautet:

»Ernst Jüngers Werk ›Der Arbeiter‹ hat Gewicht, weil es, auf eine andere Art wie Spengler, das leistet, was bisher alle Nietzsche-Literatur nicht vermochte, nämlich eine Erfahrung des Seienden und dessen, wie es ist, im Lichte von Nietzsches Entwurf des Seienden als Wille zur Macht zu vermitteln. Frei-

first is only European, appears in its planetary tendency. However, there is no description in itself which would be able to show reality in itself. Every description, the more sharply it advances, moves that much more positively in its own way within a definite horizon. The manner of vision and the horizon—you say "optics"—appear for human conceptions from the basic experiences of being in the whole. But they are already proceeded by a vista never to be made first by man, of how being "is." The basic experience which carries and pervades your conception and presentation arose in the destructiveness of the first World War. Being in the whole, however, reveals itself to you in the light and shadow of the metaphysics of the will to power which Nietzsche expounds in the form of a doctrine of values.

In the winter of 1939 to 1940 I explained *The Worker* in a small circle of university professors. They were astonished that such a clear-sighted book had been available for years and that no one had yet learned by himself to dare make the attempt to let his glance move towards the present in the optics of the *Worker* and to do some planetary thinking. It was felt that to do this even the universally historical view of world history did not suffice. In those days the *Marble Cliffs* was much read but, as it seemed to me, without an adequately broad, that is, planetary horizon. There was, however, also no surprise that an attempt to explain the *Worker* was being watched and was finally forbidden. For it is a part of the essence of the will to power not to permit the reality which it has power over to appear in *that* reality in which it itself exists.

You will permit me to repeat a review of the above-named attempt at explanation. I am doing it because I hope that in this letter I am going to be able to say some things more plainly and more freely. The review reads:

"Ernst Jünger's essay *The Worker* has weight because, in a way different from Spengler's, it achieves what all the Nietzsche literature was not able to achieve so far, namely, to communicate an experience of being and of what it is, in the light of Nietzsche's outline of being as the will to power. To be sure, Nietz-

lich ist damit Nietzsches Metaphysik keineswegs denkerisch begriffen; nicht einmal die Wege dahin sind gewiesen; im Gegenteil: statt im echten Sinne fragwürdig, wird diese Metaphysik selbstverständlich und scheinbar überflüssig.«

Sie sehen, die kritische Frage denkt in einer Hinsicht, die zu
verfolgen allerdings nicht in den Aufgabenkreis der Beschreibungen gehört, die »Der Arbeiter« durchführt. Vieles von dem,
was Ihre Beschreibungen in den Blick und erstmals zur Sprache
brachten, sieht und sagt heute jedermann. Überdies verdankt
»Die Frage nach der Technik« den Beschreibungen im »Arbeiter« eine nachhaltige Förderung. Hinsichtlich Ihrer »Beschreibungen« sei der Vermerk angebracht, daß sie nicht ein schon
bekanntes Wirkliches nur abschildern, sondern eine »neue
Wirklichkeit« zugänglich machen, wobei es sich »weniger um
neue Gedanken oder ein neues System handelt . . .« (Der Arbeiter, Vorwort).

Auch heute noch – wie sollte es nicht – sammelt sich das Frucht-
bare Ihres Sagens in der wohlverstandenen »Beschreibung«.
Doch sind Optik und Gesichtskreis, die das Beschreiben leiten,
nicht mehr oder noch nicht entsprechend bestimmt wie vormals.
Denn Sie nehmen jetzt an jener Aktion des aktiven Nihilismus
nicht mehr teil, die auch im »Arbeiter« schon nach dem Sinne
Nietzsches in der Richtung auf eine Überwindung gedacht ist.
Nichtmehrteilnehmen heißt jedoch keineswegs schon: außerhalb
des Nihilismus stehen, zumal dann nicht, wenn das Wesen des
Nihilismus nichts Nihilistisches und die Geschichte dieses Wesens älter ist und jünger bleibt als die historisch feststellbaren
Phasen der verschiedenen Formen des Nihilismus. Darum gehört
auch Ihr Werk »Der Arbeiter« und die ihm nachfolgende, noch
weiter vorspringende Abhandlung »Über den Schmerz« (1934)
nicht zu den abgelegten Akten der nihilistischen Bewegung. Im
Gegenteil: mir scheint, diese Werke *bleiben,* weil sich an ihnen,
insofern sie die Sprache unseres Jahrhunderts sprechen, die
noch keineswegs geleistete Auseinandersetzung mit dem
Wesen des Nihilismus neu entzünden kann.

Während ich dies schreibe, erinnere ich unser Gespräch gegen Ende des vorigen Jahrzehnts. Beim Gang auf einem Wald-
weg hielten wir an einer Stelle inne, wo ein Holzweg abzweigt.

sche's metaphysics has thereby by no means been speculatively understood; not even the paths towards it are indicated; on the contrary, instead of being questionable, in the true sense of the word, this metaphysics becomes a matter of course and apparently superfluous."

You see, the critical question thinks in a sense which, to be sure, it is not within the province of the descriptions achieved by *The Worker* to pursue. Much of what your descriptions brought into view and discussed for the first time, everyone sees and says today. Besides, *The Question about Technology* owes enduring advancement to the descriptions in *The Worker*. In regard to your "descriptions" it might be appropriate to remark that you do not merely depict something real that is already known but make available a "new reality" in which it is "less a question of new ideas or of a new system . . ." (*The Worker,* Foreword).

But even today—and why should it not be so?—what is fruitful in what you say is gathered together in the well-understood "description." However, the optics and the horizon which guide the describing are no longer or not yet correspondingly determined as they were formerly. For now you no longer take part in the action of active nihilism, which is also already thought of in *The Worker* in Nietzsche's sense in the direction towards an overcoming. No longer taking part, however, by no means already means standing outside of nihilism, especially not when the essence of nihilism is not nihilistic and the history of this essence is older and yet remains younger than the historically determinable phases of the various forms of nihilism. Therefore, your essay *The Worker* and the succeeding even more advanced treatise, *About Pain* (1934) do not belong among the discarded documents of the nihilistic movement. On the contrary, it seems to me that these works will *last* because by them, insofar as they speak the language of our century, the discussion of the *essence* of nihilism, which has by no means yet been accomplished, can be newly enkindled.

While I am writing this I recall our conversation towards the end of the last decade. On a walk along a forest road we stopped at a place where a woodland path branches off. At that time I

Damals ermunterte ich Sie, den »Arbeiter« wieder und zwar unverändert erscheinen zu lassen. Sie folgten diesem Vorschlag nur zögernd aus Gründen, die weniger den Inhalt des Buches als den rechten Augenblick seines Wiedererscheinens betrafen. Unser Gespräch über den »Arbeiter« brach ab. Ich selbst war auch nicht gesammelt genug, um die Gründe meines Vorschlages hinreichend klar auseinanderzulegen. Inzwischen dürfte die Zeit reifer geworden sein, um davon einiges zu sagen.

Einerseits ist die Bewegung des Nihilismus in ihrer planetarischen und alles anzehrenden, vielgestaltigen Unaufhaltsamkeit offenkundiger geworden. Kein Einsichtiger wird heute noch leugnen wollen, daß der Nihilismus in den verschiedensten und verstecktesten Gestalten der »Normalzustand« der Menschheit ist (vgl. Nietzsche, Wille zur Macht, Nr. 23). Am besten zeugen dafür die ausschließlich re-aktiven Versuche gegen den Nihilismus, die, statt auf eine Auseinandersetzung mit seinem Wesen sich einzulassen, die Restauration des Bisherigen betreiben. Sie suchen die Rettung in der Flucht, nämlich in der Flucht vor dem Einblick in die Fragwürdigkeit der metaphysischen Position des Menschen. Dieselbe Flucht drängt auch dort, wo man dem Anschein nach alle Metaphysik aufgibt und sie durch Logistik, Soziologie und Psychologie ersetzt. Der hier vorbrechende Wille zum Wissen und dessen lenkbarer Gesamtorganisation deutet auf eine Steigerung des Willens zur Macht, die anderer Art ist als jene, die Nietzsche als aktiven Nihilismus kennzeichnete.

Andererseits sinnt jetzt Ihr eigenes Dichten und Trachten darauf, aus der Zone des vollendeten Nihilismus herauszuhelfen, ohne daß Sie den Grundriß der Perspektive aufgeben, die »Der Arbeiter« von Nietzsches Metaphysik her öffnete.

Sie schreiben (Über die Linie, S. 36): »Die Totale Mobilmachung ist in ein Stadium eingetreten, das an Bedrohlichkeit noch das vergangene übertrifft. Der Deutsche freilich ist nicht mehr ihr Subjekt, und dadurch wächst die Gefahr, daß er als ihr Objekt begriffen wird.« Auch jetzt noch sehen Sie und zwar mit Recht die Totale Mobilmachung als einen auszeichnenden Charakter des Wirklichen. Aber dessen Wirklichkeit ist für Sie jetzt nicht mehr durch den *»Willen zur* (von mir ge-

urged you to have *The Worker* republished unchanged. You followed my suggestion only reluctantly for reasons which were concerned less with the content of the book than with the proper moment of its reappearance. Our conversation about *The Worker* was broken off. My own thoughts were not sufficiently collected in order to analyze clearly enough the reasons for my proposal. In the meanwhile, time has probably become riper so that I may say something about it.

On the one hand, the movement of nihilism has become more manifest in its planetary, all-corroding, many-faceted irresistibleness. No one with any insight will still deny today that nihilism is in the most varied and most hidden forms of "the normal state" of man (cf. Nietzsche, *Will to Power*, No. 23). The best evidences of this are the exclusively re-active attempts against nihilism, which, instead of entering into a discussion of its essence, strive for the restoration of what has been. They seek salvation in flight, namely in flight from a glimpse of the worthiness of questioning the metaphysical position of man. The same flight is also urgent where apparently all metaphysics is abandoned and is replaced by logistics, sociology, and psychology. The will to know which breaks forth here, and its more tractable total organization, points to an increase of the will to power, which is of a different kind from that which Nietzsche designated as active nihilism.

On the other hand, your own thoughts and desires are aimed at helping to get out of the zone of complete nihilism without giving up the groundplan of the prospect which *The Worker*, preceding from Nietzsche's metaphysics, opened up.

You write (*Across the Line*, p. 36): 'Total mobilization has entered a stage which is even more threatening than what has gone before. The German is, to be sure, no longer its subject, and thereby the danger grows that he will be conceived as its object." Even now you see total mobilization, and rightly so, as a distinguishing character of what is real. But its reality is for you no longer determined by the "*will to* (the italics are mine) total

sperrt) Totalen Mobilmachung« (Der Arbeiter, S. 148) bestimmt und nicht mehr so, daß dieser Wille als die einzige Quelle der alles rechtfertigenden »Sinngebung« gelten darf. Darum schreiben Sie (Über die Linie, S. 30): »Es ist kein Zweifel daran, daß unser Bestand (d. h. nach S. 31 »die Personen, Werke und Einrichtungen«) als Ganzes sich über die kritische Linie bewegt. Damit verändern sich Gefahren und Sicherheit.« In der Zone der Linie nähert sich der Nihilismus seiner Vollendung. Das Ganze des »menschlichen Bestandes« kann die Linie nur dann überqueren, wenn dieser Bestand aus der Zone des vollendeten Nihilismus heraustritt.

Demgemäß muß eine Erörterung der Linie fragen: worin besteht die Vollendung des Nihilismus? Die Antwort scheint nahe zu liegen. Der Nihilismus ist vollendet, wenn er alle Bestände ergriffen hat und überall auftritt, wenn nichts mehr als Ausnahme sich behaupten kann, insofern er zum Normalzustand geworden ist. Doch im Normalzustand *verwirklicht* sich nur die Vollendung. Jener ist eine Folge dieser. Vollendung meint die Versammlung aller Wesensmöglichkeiten des Nihilismus, die im ganzen und im einzelnen schwer durchschaubar bleiben. Die Wesensmöglichkeiten des Nihilismus lassen sich nur bedenken, wenn wir auf sein Wesen zurückdenken. Ich sage »zurück«, weil das Wesen des Nihilismus den einzelnen nihilistischen Erscheinungen vorauf- und deshalb vorauswährt und sie in die Vollendung versammelt. Die Vollendung des Nihilismus ist jedoch nicht schon dessen Ende. Mit der Vollendung des Nihilismus *beginnt* erst die Endphase des Nihilismus. Deren Zone ist vermutlich, weil sie von einem Normalzustand und dessen Verfestigung durchherrscht wird, ungewöhnlich breit. Deshalb ist die Null-Linie, wo die Vollendung zum Ende wird, am Ende noch gar nicht sichtbar.

Wie steht es aber dann mit der Aussicht auf ein Überqueren der Linie? Ist der menschliche Bestand schon im Übergang trans lineam oder betritt er erst das weite Vorfeld vor der Linie? Vielleicht bannt uns aber auch eine unvermeidliche Augentäuschung. Vielleicht taucht die Null-Linie in der Form einer planetarischen Katastrophe jäh vor uns auf. Wer überquert sie dann noch? Und was vermögen Katastrophen? Die

mobilization" (*The Worker*, p. 148) and no longer in such a way that this will may be regarded as the only source of the "giving of meaning" which justifies everything. That is why you write (*Across the Line*, p. 30): "There is no doubt that our component realities (these are, according to p. 31 "personnel, works, and installations") as a whole are moving across the critical line. Thereby dangers and security are changing." In the zone of the line, nihilism approaches its completion. The totality of the "human component realities" can only cross over the line when they step out of the zone of complete nihilism.

Accordingly, a discussion of the line must ask in what the fulfillment of nihilism consists. The answer seems to be obvious. Nihilism is fulfilled when it has seized all the component realities and appears everywhere, when nothing can assert itself any longer as an exception, in so far as it has become a normal state. However, it is only in the normal state that the fulfillment *is realized*. The former is a consequence of the latter. Fulfillment means the gathering together of all the possibilities of the essence of nihilism which as a whole and individually remain difficult to see through. The possibilities of the essence of nihilism can only be considered if we think back to its essence. I say "back" because the essence of nihilism comes before and, therefore, ahead of each of the nihilistic phenomena and collects them in its fulfillmnt. The fulfillment of nihilism is, however, not already its end. With the fulfillment of nihilism only *begins* the final phase of nihilism. Its zone, because it is dominated throughout by a normal state and its consolidation, is presumably unusually broad. That is why the zero-line, where fulfillment approaches the end, is not yet at all visible at the end.

What is the situation, however, with regard to the prospect of a crossing of the line? Are the human component realities already in transit *trans lineam* or are they only entering the wide field in front of the line? But perhaps we are being held spellbound by an unavoidable optical delusion. Perhaps the zero-line is suddenly emerging before us in the form of a planetary catastrophe. Who will then still cross it? And what can catastrophes do? The

zwei Weltkriege haben die Bewegung des Nihilismus weder aufgehalten, noch aus ihrer Richtung abgelenkt. Was Sie (S. 36) über die Totale Mobilmachung sagen, gibt die Bestätigung. Wie steht es jetzt mit der kritischen Linie? In jedem Falle so, daß eine Erörterung ihres Ortes eine Besinnung darüber erwecken könnte, ob und inwiefern wir an ein Überqueren der Linie denken dürfen.

Allein der Versuch, im Briefgespräch mit Ihnen einiges de linea zu sagen, trifft auf eine eigentümliche Schwierigkeit. Deren Grund liegt darin, daß Sie im »Hinüber« über die Linie, d. h. im Raum diesseits und jenseits der Linie, die gleiche Sprache sprechen. Die Position des Nihilismus ist, so scheint es, in gewisser Weise durch das Überqueren der Linie schon aufgegeben, aber *seine Sprache ist geblieben*. Ich meine hier die Sprache nicht als bloßes Ausdrucksmittel, das sich wie eine Verkleidung ablegen und auswechseln läßt, ohne daß jenes, was zur Sprache gekommen ist, davon berührt wird. In der Sprache erscheint allererst und west jenes, was wir bei der Verwendung maßgebender Worte anscheinend nur nachträglich aussprechen und zwar in Ausdrücken, von denen wir meinen, sie könnten beliebig wegfallen und durch andere ersetzt werden. Die Sprache im »Arbeiter« offenbart ihre Hauptzüge, wie mir scheint, am ehesten im Untertitel des Werkes. Er heißt: »Herrschaft und Gestalt«. Er kennzeichnet den Grundriß des Werkes. »Gestalt« verstehen Sie zunächst im Sinne der damaligen Gestaltpsychologie als »ein Ganzes, das mehr als die Summe seiner Teile umfaßt.« Man könnte bedenken, inwiefern diese Kennzeichnung der Gestalt sich immer noch, nämlich durch das »mehr« und »die Summe«, an das summative Vorstellen anlehnt und das Gestalthafte als solches im Unbestimmten läßt. Aber Sie geben der Gestalt einen kultischen Rang und setzen sie dadurch mit Recht gegen die »bloße Idee« ab.

Hierbei ist die »Idee« neuzeitlich im Sinne der perceptio, des Vorstellens durch ein Subjekt, verstanden. Andererseits bleibt auch für Sie die Gestalt nur in einem Sehen zugänglich. Es ist jenes Sehen, das bei den Griechen ἰδεῖν heißt, welches Wort Platon für ein Blicken gebraucht, das nicht das sinnlich

two World Wars neither checked the movement of nihilism nor diverted it from its course. What you say (p. 36) about total mobilization provides the confirmation. How do matters stand now with the critical line? In every case they stand in such a way that a discussion of its place might arouse a consideration of whether and in what way we may think of a crossing of the line.

However, the attempt to say a few things in a conversation with you by letter encounters a peculiar difficulty. The reason for it lies in the fact that in the "beyond" across the line, that is, in the space on this side of and on the other side of the line, you speak the same language. The position of nihilism has, so it seems, already been given up in a certain way by the crossing of the line, but *its language has remained.* Here I mean language not as a mere means of expression, which can be taken off and changed like clothing without touching that which is being discussed. In language there appears first of all and exists that which in the use of suitable words we apparently only express subsequently and, what is more, with expressions which we believe might be omitted at will and be replaced by others. The language in *The Worker* reveals its chief features, it seems to me, first and foremost in the subtitle of the work. It reads "Dominance and *Gestalt.*" It characterizes the basic outline of the work. "*Gestalt*" you understand first in the sense of the *Gestalt* psychology of that time as "a whole which comprises more than the sum of its parts." One might consider to what extent this characterization of *Gestalt* still, namely through the "more" and "the sum," leans on summative conception and leaves what is form-like as such in uncertainty. But you put *Gestalt* on a cultist level and thereby rightly set it off against "mere idea."

Here "idea" is understood in the modern sense of *perceptio,* of perception through a subject. On the other hand, for you too, form is accessible only through seeing. It is that kind of seeing which the Greeks call *idein,* a word which Plato uses for a seeing which does not see that changeable thing which is perceivable

wahrnehmbare Veränderliche, sondern das Unveränderliche, das Sein, die ἰδέα erblickt. Auch Sie kennzeichnen die Gestalt als »ruhendes Sein«. Die Gestalt ist zwar keine »Idee« im neuzeitlichen Verstande, darum auch keine regulative Vorstellung der Vernunft im Sinne Kants. Das ruhende Sein bleibt für das griechische Denken rein unterschieden (different) gegenüber dem veränderlichen Seienden. Diese Differenz zwischen Sein und Seiendem erscheint dann, vom Seienden zum Sein hin erblickt, als die Transzendenz, d. h. als das Meta-Physische. Allein die Unterscheidung ist keine absolute Trennung. Sie ist es so wenig, daß im Anwesen (Sein) das An-wesende (Seiende) her-vor-gebracht, aber gleichwohl nicht verursacht wird im Sinne einer efficienten Kausalität. Das Her-vor-bringende ist von Platon bisweilen als das Prägende (τύπος) gedacht (vgl. Theätet 192 a, 194 b). Auch Sie denken die Beziehung der Gestalt zu dem, was sie »gestaltet«, als das Verhältnis von Stempel und Prägung. Allerdings verstehen Sie das Prägen neuzeitlich als ein Verleihen von »Sinn« an das Sinn-lose. Die Gestalt ist »Quelle der Sinngebung« (Der Arbeiter, S. 148).

Der geschichtliche Hinweis auf die Zusammengehörigkeit von Gestalt, ἰδέα und Sein möchte Ihr Werk nicht historisch verrechnen, sondern anzeigen, *daß es in der Metaphysik beheimatet bleibt.* Dieser gemäß ist alles Seiende, das veränderliche und bewegte, mobile und mobilisierte von einem »ruhenden Sein« her vorgestellt, dies auch dort noch, wo, wie bei Hegel und Nietzsche, das »Sein« (die Wirklichkeit des Wirklichen) als reines Werden und absolute Bewegtheit gedacht wird. Die Gestalt ist »metaphysische Macht« (Der Arbeiter, S. 113, 124, 146).

Nach anderer Hinsicht unterscheidet sich jedoch das metaphysische Vorstellen im »Arbeiter« vom platonischen und sogar vom neuzeitlichen, dasjenige Nietzsches ausgenommen. Die Quelle der Sinngebung, die im vorhinein präsente und so alles prägende Macht, ist die Gestalt als Gestalt eines *Menschentums:* »Die Gestalt des Arbeiters«. Die Gestalt ruht im Wesensgefüge eines Menschentums, das als Subiectum allem Seienden zugrundeliegt. Nicht die Ichheit eines vereinzelten Menschen, das Subjektive der Egoität, sondern die vor-

through the senses but that unchangeable thing, Being, the idea. You also characterize *Gestalt* as "Being in repose." *Gestalt* is, to be sure, not an "idea" in the modern sense of the word, but for that reason it is also not a regulative conception of rea- son in the Kantian sense. Being in repose remains for Greek thinking utterly different from changeable being. This difference between Being and being then appears, as seen in the direction from being to Being, as transcendence, that is, as the meta-physi- cal. However, this difference is not an absolute separation. So little, indeed, that what is present (being) is brought forth in the present (Being) but is, however, not caused by it, in the sense of an efficient causation. That which brings forth is at times thought of by Plato as that which makes an imprint (*tupos*) (cf. Theätet 192 a, 194 b). You also think of the relationship of form to that which "forms" it as the relationship between stamp and impression. To be sure, you understand the stamping in the modern sense as bestowing "meaning" on the meaning-less. *Gestalt* is the "source of bestowing of meaning" (*The Worker*, p. 148).

The historical reference to the homogeneousness of *Gestalt*, *idea*, and Being does not wish to subject your work to an histori- cal accounting, but to announce that *it dwells in metaphysics*. According to the latter, all being, the changeable and fluid, the mobile and mobilized, has been conceived as coming from a "Being in repose," even where "Being" (the reality of the real), is thought of as by Hegel and Nietzsche, as pure growth and absolute movement. *Gestalt* is "metaphysical power" (*The Work- er*, pp. 113, 124, 146).

In another respect the metaphysical conception in *The Worker* is, however, differentiated from the Platonic and even from the modern, except that of Nietzsche. The source of the giving of meaning, the power which is present from the outset and thus stamping everything, is *Gestalt* as the *Gestalt* of *a humanity:* "The *Gestalt* of the worker." *Gestalt* reposes in the essential structure of a humanity, which as subject is the basis of all being. Not the I-ness of an individual person, the subjectiveness of the egoity, but the

geformte gestalthafte Praesenz eines Menschenschlages (Typus) bildet die äußerste Subjektität, die in der Vollendung der neuzeitlichen Metaphysik hervorkommt und durch deren Denken dargestellt wird.

In der Gestalt des Arbeiters und ihrer Herrschaft ist nicht mehr die subjektive, geschweige denn die subjektivistische Subjektität des Menschenwesens erblickt. Das metaphysische Sehen der Gestalt des Arbeiters entspricht dem Entwurf der Wesensgestalt des Zarathustra innerhalb der Metaphysik des Willens zur Macht. Was verbirgt sich in diesem Erscheinen der objektiven Subjektität des Subiectum (des Seins des Seienden), das als Menschengestalt, nicht als ein einzelner Mensch gemeint ist?

Die Rede von der Subjektität (nicht Subjektivität) des Menschenwesens als dem Fundament für die Objektivität jedes Subiectum (jedes Anwesenden) scheint in aller Hinsicht paradox und gekünstelt zu sein. Dieser Anschein hat darin seinen Grund, daß wir kaum begonnen haben zu fragen, weshalb und auf welche Weise innerhalb der neuzeitlichen Metaphysik ein Denken notwendig wird, das Zarathustra als Gestalt vorstellt. Die oft gegebene Auskunft, Nietzsches Denken sei fatalerweise ins Dichten geraten, ist selbst nur die Preisgabe des denkenden Fragens. Indes brauchen wir nicht einmal bis zu Kants transzendentaler Deduktion der Kategorien zurückzudenken, um zu sehen, daß es sich beim Erblicken der Gestalt als der Quelle der Sinngebung um die *Legitimation* des Seins des Seienden handelt. Es wäre eine allzu grobe Erklärung, wollte man sagen, hier rücke in einer säkularisierten Welt der Mensch als Urheber des Seins des Seienden an die Stelle Gottes. Daß freilich das Menschenwesen im Spiel ist, duldet keinen Zweifel. Aber das Wesen (verbal) des Menschen, »das Dasein im Menschen« (vgl. Kant und das Problem der Metaphysik, 1. Aufl. 1929, § 43) ist nichts Menschliches. Damit die idea des Menschenwesens in den Rang dessen gelangen kann, was allem Anwesenden schon zum Grunde liegt als die Praesenz, die erst eine »Repräsentation« im Seienden verstattet und dieses so *als* das Seiende »legitimiert«, muß der Mensch allererst im Sinne eines maßgebenden Zugrunde-

pre-formed formlike presence of a species of men (type) forms the most extreme subjectivity which comes forth in the fulfillment of modern metaphysics and is presented by its thinking.

In the *Gestalt* of the worker and in its dominance the subjective is no longer seen, and even less, the subjectivistic subjecticity of the essence of man. The metaphysical seeing of the *Gestalt* of the worker corresponds to the outline of the essential *Gestalt* of Zarathustra within the metaphysics of the will to power. What is hidden in this appearing of the objective subjecticity of the subject (of the Being of being) which is meant as a human *Gestalt* and not as an individual human being?

Talk of the subjecticity (not subjectivity) of the essence of man as the foundation for the objectivity of every subject (everything which is present) seems to be paradoxical and artificial in every respect. The reason why this appears to be so is that we have scarcely begun to ask why and in which way within modern metaphysics a line of thinking becomes necessary which presents Zarathustra as a *Gestalt*. The oft-given statement that Nietzsche's thinking had fatally turned into imagining is itself only the abandonment of thoughtful questioning. However, we do not even have to think back as far as Kant's transcendental deduction of categories in order to see that in the process of seeing *Gestalt* as the source of the giving-of-meaning, it is a question of the *legitimation* of the Being of being. It would be an all too crude statement to say that here man moves in a secularized world in place of God as the creator of the Being of being. That the essence of man does, indeed, play a part is certain. But the being (verbal) of man, "the reality in man" (cf. Kant and *The Problem of Metaphysics,* 1st edit. 1929, § 43) is nothing human. In order that the idea of the essence of man can reach the level of that which already is the basis of everything present as being in the state of presence which first permits a "representation" in being and thus "legitimizes" it *as* being, man must first of all be represented in the sense of an authoritative funda-

liegenden vorgestellt sein. Doch maßgebend wofür? Für die Sicherung des Seienden in seinem Sein. In welchem Sinne erscheint »Sein«, wenn es um die Sicherung des Seienden geht? Im Sinne des überall und jederzeit Fest- und d. h. Vorstellbaren. Descartes fand, das Sein also verstehend, die Subjektität des Subiectum im ego cogito des endlichen Menschen. Das Erscheinen der metaphysischen Gestalt des Menschen als Quelle der Sinngebung ist die letzte Folge der Ansetzung des Menschenwesens als des maßgebenden Subiectum. Demzufolge wandelt sich die innere Form der Metaphysik, die in dem beruht, was man die Transzendenz nennen kann. Diese ist innerhalb der Metaphysik aus Wesensgründen mehrdeutig. Wo diese Mehrdeutigkeit nicht beachtet wird, macht sich eine heillose Verwirrung breit, die als das Kennzeichen des heute noch üblichen metaphysischen Vorstellens gelten darf.

Die Transzendenz ist einmal die vom Seienden aus auf das *Sein* hinübergehende Beziehung zwischen beiden. Transzendenz ist aber zugleich die vom veränderlichen Seienden zu einem *ruhenden Seienden* führende Beziehung. Transzendenz heißt schließlich, entsprechend dem Gebrauch des Titels »Excellenz«, jenes *höchste Seiende selbst,* das dann auch »das Sein« genannt wird, woraus sich eine seltsame Vermischung mit der zuerst angeführten Bedeutung ergibt.

Wozu langweile ich Sie mit dem Hinweis auf die heute allzu großzügig gehandhabten, d. h. in ihrer Verschiedenheit und Zusammengehörigkeit kaum durchdachten Unterscheidungen? Um von hier aus deutlich zu machen, wie das Meta-Physische der Metaphysik, die Transzendenz, sich wandelt, wenn in deren Unterscheidungsbereich *die Gestalt* des Menschenwesens als Quelle der Sinngebung erscheint. Die Transzendenz, in dem mehrfältigen Sinne verstanden, kehrt sich um in die entsprechende Reszendenz und verschwindet in dieser. Der so geartete Rückstieg durch die Gestalt geschieht auf die Weise, daß ihre Praesenz sich repraesentiert, im Geprägten ihrer Prägung wieder anwesend wird. Die Praesenz der Gestalt des Arbeiters ist die Macht. Die Repraesentation der Praesenz ist seine Herrschaft als ein »neuartiger und besonderer Wille zur Macht« (Der Arbeiter, S. 70).

mental. But authoritative for what? For the assuring of being in its Being. In what sense does "Being" appear if it is a question of the assuring of being? In the sense of what is everywhere and at all times determinable and, that means, representable. Understanding Being in this way, Descartes found the subjecticity of the subject in the *ego cogito* of mortal man. The appearing of the metaphysical *Gestalt* of man as the source of the giving-of-meaning is the final consequence of establishing the essence of man as its authoritative subject. Accordingly the inner form of metaphysics, which is based on what may be called transcendence, is changed. For essential reasons the latter has several meanings within metaphysics. Whenever this multiplicity of meanings is disregarded a fatal confusion spreads which may be regarded as the distinguishing characteristic of metaphysical conceptions still customary today.

Transcendence is firstly the relationship between being and Being starting from the former and going towards the latter. Transcendence is, however, at the same time the relationship leading from the changeable being to a *being in repose*. Transcendence, finally, corresponding to the use of the title "Excellency," is that *highest being itself* which can then also be called "Being," from which results a strange mixture with the first mentioned meaning.

Why do I bore you with a reference to the distinctions which are applied on much too grand a scale today, that is, scarcely thought through in their differentiation and their homogeneousness? In order to make plain from this point how the meta-physical of metaphysics, transcendence, changes, when, within the confines of the differentiation, the *Gestalt* of the essence of man appears as the source of the giving-of-meaning. Transcendence, understood in the manifold sense, turns back into the corresponding re-scendence and disappears in it. A retreat of this kind through *Gestalt* takes place in such a way that its state of being present is represented and is present again in the imprint of its stamping. The state of being of the *Gestalt* of the worker is power. The representation of the state of being present is its dominance as a "new and special kind of will to power" (*The Worker*, p. 70).

Das Neuartige und Besondere haben Sie in der »Arbeit« als dem totalen Charakter der Wirklichkeit des Wirklichen erfahren und erkannt. Dadurch wird das metaphysische Vorstellen im Lichte des Willens zur Macht entschiedener aus dem biologisch-anthropologischen Bezirk herausgedreht, der Nietzsches Weg allzu stark beirrte, was eine Aufzeichnung wie die folgende belegen mag: »Welche werden sich als die *Stärksten* dabei erweisen? (bei der Heraufkunft der Lehre von der ewigen Wiederkehr des Gleichen) ... – Menschen, die *ihrer Macht sicher sind* und die die *erreichte* Kraft des Menschen mit bewußtem Stolz repräsentiren« (Wille zur Macht, Nr. 55 Ende). »Herrschaft« ist (Der Arbeiter, S. 192) »heute nur möglich als Repräsentation der Gestalt des Arbeiters, die Anspruch auf planetarische Gültigkeit stellt.« »Arbeit« im höchsten und alle Mobilmachung durchwaltenden Sinne ist »Repräsentation der Gestalt des Arbeiters« (a. a. O. S. 202). »Die Art und Weise aber, wie die Gestalt des Arbeiters die Welt zu durchdringen beginnt, ist der totale Arbeitscharakter« (a. a. O. S. 99). Fast gleichlautend folgt später (a. a. O. S. 150) der Satz: »Die Technik ist die Art und Weise, in der die Gestalt des Arbeiters die Welt mobilisiert.«

Unmittelbar vorauf geht die entscheidende Bemerkung: »Um zur Technik ein wirkliches Verhältnis zu besitzen, muß man etwas mehr als Techniker sein« (a. a. O. S. 149). Den Satz kann ich nur so verstehen: mit dem »wirklichen« Verhältnis meinen Sie das wahre Verhältnis. Wahr ist jenes, das dem Wesen der Technik entspricht. Durch das unmittelbar technische Leisten, d. h. durch den jeweils speziellen Arbeitscharakter wird dieses Wesensverhältnis nie erreicht. Es beruht in der Beziehung zum totalen Arbeitscharakter. Die so verstandene »Arbeit« ist jedoch mit dem Sein im Sinne des Willens zur Macht identisch (a. a. O. S. 86).

Welche Wesensbestimmung der Technik ergibt sich hieraus? Sie ist »das Symbol der Gestalt des Arbeiters« (a. a. O. S. 72). Die Technik gründet »als Mobilisierung der Welt durch die Gestalt des Arbeiters« (a. a. O. S. 154) offenbar in jener Umkehrung der Transzendenz zur Reszendenz der Gestalt des Arbeiters, wodurch deren Praesenz sich in die Repraesenta-

This new and special characteristic you have become aware of and have recognized in "work" as the total character of the reality of the real. Thereby metaphysical conception, in the light of the will to power, is wrested more decidedly out of the biological-anthropological range which confused Nietzsche's path too much, evidence of which may be found in a remark such as the following: "Which ones will prove to be the *strongest* in this? (in the rise of the doctrine of the eternal recurrence of the identical) . . .—Men, who *are sure of their power* and who represent with conscious pride the *achieved* strength of man (*Will to Power*, No. 55 end). "Dominance" (*The Worker*, p. 192) is "only possible today as the representation of the *Gestalt* of the worker which lays claim to planetary validity." "Work" in the highest sense and in the sense which permeates all mobilization is "representation of the *Gestalt* of the worker" (*Ibid.*, p. 202). "However, the way in which the *Gestalt* of the worker is beginning to penetrate the world is the total character of work" (*Ibid.*, p. 99). A later sentence (p. 150) reads almost the same: "Technology is the way in which the *Gestalt* of the worker mobilizes the world."

Directly ahead of this is the decisive remark: "In order to have a real relationship to technology one must be something more than a technician" (p. 149). That statement I can only understand in this way: by "real" relationship you mean true relationship. True is that which corresponds to the essence of technology. Through direct technical achievement, that is, through the at times special character of work, this fundamental relationship is never attained. It rests on the relationship to the total character of work. "Work" understood in this way is, however, identical with Being in the sense of the will to power (p. 86).

Which definition of the essence of technology results from this? It is "the symbol of the *Gestalt* of the worker" (p. 72). Technology is obviously based, "as mobilization of the world through the *Gestalt* of the worker" (p. 154), on that reversal of transcendence into the re-scendence of the *Gestalt* of the worker whereby its state of being present is developed into the representation of its

tion ihrer Macht entfaltet. Darum können Sie (a. a. O.) schreiben: »Die Technik ist ... wie die Zerstörerin jedes Glaubens überhaupt, so auch die entschiedenste antichristliche Macht, die bisher in Erscheinung getreten ist.«

Ihr Werk »Der Arbeiter« zeichnet bereits durch seinen Untertitel »Herrschaft und Gestalt« die Grundzüge jener im ganzen hervortretenden neuen Metaphysik des Willens zur Macht vor, insofern dieser sich jetzt überall und vollständig als Arbeit praesentiert. Schon beim ersten Lesen dieses Werkes bewegten mich die Fragen, die ich auch heute noch vorbringen muß: woher bestimmt sich das Wesen der Arbeit? Ergibt es sich aus der Gestalt des Arbeiters? Wodurch ist die Gestalt eine solche des Arbeiters, wenn nicht das Wesen der Arbeit sie durchwaltet? Empfängt sonach diese Gestalt ihre menschentümliche Praesenz aus dem Wesen der Arbeit? Woher ergibt sich der Sinn von Arbeiten und Arbeiter in dem hohen Rang, den Sie der Gestalt und ihrer Herrschaft zusprechen? Entspringt dieser Sinn daraus, daß Arbeit hier als eine Prägung des Willens zur Macht gedacht ist? Stammt diese Besonderung gar aus dem Wesen der Technik »als der Mobilisierung der Welt durch die Gestalt des Arbeiters«? Und verweist schließlich das so bestimmte Wesen der Technik in noch ursprünglichere Bereiche?

Allzu leicht könnte man darauf hinweisen, daß in Ihren Darlegungen über das Verhältnis zwischen dem totalen Arbeitscharakter und der Gestalt des Arbeiters ein Zirkel das Bestimmende (die Arbeit) und das Bestimmte (den Arbeiter) in ihre wechselseitige Beziehung verklammert. Statt diesen Hinweis als Beleg für ein unlogisches Denken auszuwerten, nehme ich den Zirkel als Zeichen dafür, daß hier das Runde eines Ganzen zu denken bleibt, in einem Denken freilich, für das eine an der Widerspruchsfreiheit gemessene »Logik« nie der Maßstab werden kann.

Die vorhin aufgeworfenen Fragen gelangen in eine noch schärfere Fragwürdigkeit, wenn ich sie so fasse, wie ich sie Ihnen unlängst im Anschluß an meinen Vortrag in München (Die Frage nach der Technik) vorlegen wollte. Wenn die Technik die Mobilisierung der Welt durch die Gestalt des Ar-

power. Therefore, you can write (*Ibid.*): "Technology . . . like the destroyer of all faith in general, is also the most decisive anti-Christian power which has appeared hitherto."

Your essay, *The Worker*, by means of its subtitle "Dominance and *Gestalt*," already outlines the characteristic features of that entire new metaphysics of the will to power, insofar as this will is now presented everywhere and completely as work. Already at the first reading of your essay I was stirred by the questions which I must still raise today: what determines the essence of work? Does it result from the *Gestalt* of the worker? How so is the *Gestalt* of the worker such as it is if the essence of work does not pervade it? Does this *Gestalt* accordingly acquire its human state of being present from the essence of work? Whence comes the meaning of working and worker at the high level which you assign to *Gestalt* and its dominance? Does this meaning originate from the fact that work is thought of here as an imprinting of the will to power? Does this particularization perhaps even stem from the essence of technology "as the mobilization of the world through the *Gestalt* of the worker"? And finally, does the essence of technology determined in this way point into even more primordial regions?

All too easily one might point out that in your delineations of the relationship between the total character of work and the *Gestalt* of the worker, a circle embraces the determining (work) and the determined (the worker) in their reciprocal relationship. Instead of evaluating this reference as a proof of illogical thinking, I take the circle as a sign that here the roundness of a whole is to be thought of, in a kind of thinking, to be sure, for which "logic," measured by the freedom of contradiction, can never be the standard.

The questions raised above are even more clearly worthy of question if I frame them as I wanted to present them to you recently in connection with my lecture in Munich (*The Question about Technology*). If technology is the mobilization of the world through the *Gestalt* of the worker, it takes place through the

beiters ist, geschieht sie durch die prägende Praesenz dieses besonderen menschentümlichen Willens zur Macht. In der Praesenz und der Repraesentation bekundet sich der Grundzug dessen, was sich dem abendländischen Denken als Sein enthüllte. »Sein« besagt seit der Frühzeit des Griechentums bis in die Spätzeit unseres Jahrhunderts: Anwesen. Jede Art von Praesenz und Praesentation entstammt dem Ereignis der Anwesenheit. Der »Wille zur Macht« aber ist als die Wirklichkeit des Wirklichen eine Weise des Erscheinens des »Seins« des Seienden. »Arbeit«, woraus die Gestalt des Arbeiters ihrerseits den Sinn empfängt, ist identisch mit »Sein«. Hier bleibt zu bedenken, ob und inwiefern das Wesen des »Seins« in sich der Bezug zum Menschenwesen ist (vgl. Was heißt Denken? S. 73 f.). In diesem Bezug müßte dann die Beziehung zwischen der metaphysisch verstandenen »Arbeit« und dem »Arbeiter« gründen. Mir scheint, die folgenden Fragen lassen sich kaum mehr umgehen:

Dürfen wir die Gestalt des Arbeiters als Gestalt, dürfen wir die $\grave{\iota}\delta\acute{\epsilon}\alpha$ Platons als $\epsilon\tilde{\iota}\delta o\varsigma$ noch ursprünglicher auf ihre Wesensherkunft bedenken? Wenn nein, welche Gründe verwehren dies und verlangen statt dessen, Gestalt und $\grave{\iota}\delta\acute{\epsilon}\alpha$ als Letztes für uns und als Erstes an sich einfach hinzunehmen? Wenn ja, auf welchen Wegen kann sich die Frage nach der Wesensherkunft der $\grave{\iota}\delta\acute{\epsilon}\alpha$ und der Gestalt bewegen? Entspringt, um es formelhaft zu sagen, das Wesen der Gestalt im Herkunftsbereich dessen, was ich das Ge-Stell nenne? Gehört demnach auch die Wesensherkunft der $\grave{\iota}\delta\acute{\epsilon}\alpha$ in den selben Bereich, aus dem das mit ihr verwandte Wesen der Gestalt stammt? Oder ist das Ge-Stell nur eine Funktion der Gestalt eines Menschentums? Wäre dies der Fall, dann bliebe das *Wesen* des Seins und vollends das Sein des Seienden ein Gemächte des menschlichen Vorstellens. Das Zeitalter, in dem europäisches Denken solches meinte, wirft noch den letzten Schatten über uns.

Zunächst bleiben diese Fragen nach Gestalt und Ge-Stell absonderliche Überlegungen. Sie sollen niemandem aufgedrängt werden, zumal sie selber sich noch im Vorläufigen abmühen. Die Fragen sind in diesem Brief auch nicht als solche vorgebracht, die im »Arbeiter« hätten gestellt werden müssen.

stamping state of being present of this special human will to power. In the state of being present and representation is manifested the characteristic trait of what was revealed to Western thought as Being. "Being" has since the early days of the Greek world up to the latest days of our century meant being present. Every kind of state of being present and presentation stems from the event of being present. The "will to power," however, as the reality of the real, is a phase of the appearance of the "Being" of being. "Work," from which the *Gestalt* of the worker for its part obtains its meaning, is identical with "Being." Here it is to be considered whether and to what extent the essence of "Being" is in itself the relation with the essence of man. (cf. *Was heisst Denken?*, p. 73f.). In this relation would then have to be based the relationship between "work," as understood metaphysically, and the "worker." It seems to me that the following questions can scarcely be avoided:

May we consider the *Gestalt* of the worker as *Gestalt;* may we consider Plato's *idea* as *eidos* even more primordially in respect to the origin of their essence? If not, which reasons forbid this and demand instead that *Gestalt* and *idea* be taken simply as the ultimate for us and the first in themselves? If so, along which paths can the question as to the origin of the essence of the *idea* and of *Gestalt* move? By way of formulation, does the essence of *Gestalt* arise in the area of origin of what I call *Ge-Stell?* Does the origin of the essence of the *idea* accordingly also belong within the same area from which comes the essence of *Gestalt* which is related to it? Or is the *Ge-Stell* only a function of the human *Gestalt?* If this were the case, then the *essence* of Being and the Being of being would be completely the making of human conception. The era in which European thinking meant this is still casting its last shadow over us.

In the first place, these questions as to *Gestalt* and *Ge-Stell* remain peculiar considerations. They should not be imposed on anyone, especially since they are themselves still struggling in a temporary state. Nor are the questions in this letter raised as such as should have been raised in *The Worker*. To demand

Dies fordern, hieße den Stil des Werkes verkennen. Was ihm obliegt, ist, die Auslegung der Wirklichkeit hinsichtlich ihres totalen Arbeitscharakters zu erbringen, so zwar, daß die Auslegung selbst an diesem Charakter teilhat und den speziellen Arbeitscharakter eines Autors in diesem Zeitalter bekundet. Darum stehen am Ende des Buches in der »Übersicht« (S. 296, Anmerkung) folgende Sätze: »Alle diese Begriffe (Gestalt, Typus, organische Konstruktion, total) sind *notabene* zum Begreifen da. Es kommt uns auf sie nicht an. Sie mögen ohne weiteres vergessen oder beiseite gestellt werden, nachdem sie als Arbeitsgrößen zur Erfassung einer bestimmten Wirklichkeit, die trotz und jenseits jedes Begriffes besteht, benutzt worden sind; der Leser hat *durch* die Beschreibung wie durch ein optisches System hindurchzusehen.«

Dieses »notabene« habe ich inzwischen jedesmal beim Lesen Ihrer Schriften befolgt und mich gefragt, ob für Sie die Begriffe, die Wortbedeutungen und vordem die Sprache nur ein »optisches System« sein können, ob diesen Systemen gegenüber eine Wirklichkeit an sich bestehe, von der die Systeme sich gleich aufgeschraubten Apparaturen wieder ab- und durch andere ersetzen ließen. Liegt es nicht schon im Sinne von »Arbeitsgrößen«, daß sie die Wirklichkeit, den totalen Arbeitscharakter alles Wirklichen je nur so mitbestimmen, wie sie selber schon durch ihn bestimmt sind? Begriffe sind allerdings »zum Be-greifen da«. Allein das neuzeitliche Vorstellen des Wirklichen, die Vergegenständigung, in der sich das Be-greifen im vorhinein bewegt, bleibt überall ein Angriff auf das Wirkliche, insofern dieses herausgefordert ist, sich im Gesichtskreis des vorstellenden Griffes zu zeigen. Die Herausforderung hat im Umkreis des neuzeitlich-modernen Be-greifens zur Folge, daß die be-griffene Wirklichkeit unversehens und doch zunächst lange Zeit unbeachtet zum Gegenangriff übergeht, von dem die moderne Naturwissenschaft plötzlich trotz Kant überrascht wird und sich diese Überraschung erst durch eigene Entdeckungen innerhalb des wissenschaftlichen Vorgehens als eine gesicherte Erkenntnis nahe bringen muß.

Die Heisenberg'sche Unbestimmtheitsrelation läßt sich gewiß nie geradehin aus Kants transzendentaler Auslegung der

this would be to misunderstand the style of the essay. It is encumbent upon it to achieve the interpretation of reality in regard to the total character of its work, in such a way, in fact, that the interpretation itself plays a part in this character and proclaims the special character of the work of an author in this day and age. That is why at the end of the book, in the "survey" (p. 296, note) there are the following sentences: "All of these concepts (*Gestalt,* type, organic construction, total) are *notabene* there by way of comprehension. We are not concerned with them as such. They can be forgotten or set aside without further ado after they have been used as magnitudes of work for the grasping of a definite reality which exists in spite of and beyond every concept; the reader has to see *through* the description as through an optical system."

This *"notabene"* I have in the meanwhile obeyed each time in reading your writings and have asked myself whether concepts, meanings of words, and, before that, language can only be an "optical system" for you, whether, facing these systems, there exists a reality in itself by which the systems, like screwed on apparatuses, can be unscrewed and replaced by others. Is it not already inherent in the meaning of "work magnitudes" that in each case they help to determine the reality, the total character of work of everything real, only in such a way as they are already determined by it? Concepts are, to be sure, "there to be grasped." However, the modern conception of what is real, the objectification in comprehending which moves from the start, always remains an attack on the real in so far as the latter is challenged to put in an appearance within the horizon of the concept. The consequence of the challenge in the environs of contemporary comprehension is that the grasped reality proceeds unexpectedly and, at first, long unnoticed, to a counter-attack by which modern natural science, in spite of Kant, is suddenly surprised and must first become acquainted with this surprise as certain knowledge by its own discoveries within the scientific process.

Heisenberg's relation of indeterminateness can certainly never be derived directly from Kant's transcendental interpretation of

physikalischen Naturerkenntnis ableiten. Aber ebensowenig kann jene Relation jemals vorgestellt, d. h. gedacht werden, ohne daß dieses Vorstellen zunächst auf den transzendentalen Bereich der Subjekt-Objekt-Beziehung zurückgeht. Wenn dies geschehen ist, dann beginnt erst die Frage nach der Wesensherkunft der Vergegenständigung des Seienden, d. h. nach dem Wesen des »Be-greifens«.

In Ihrem und in meinem Fall handelt es sich jedoch nicht einmal nur um Begriffe einer Wissenschaft, sondern um Grundworte wie Gestalt, Herrschaft, Repräsentation, Macht, Wille, Wert, Sicherheit, um die Praesenz (Anwesen) und das Nichts, das als die Absenz der Praesenz Abbruch tut (»nichtet«), ohne sie jemals zu vernichten. Insofern das Nichts »nichtet«, bestätigt es sich vielmehr als eine ausgezeichnete Praesenz, verschleiert es sich als diese selbst. In den genannten Grundworten waltet ein anderes Sagen als das wissenschaftliche Aussagen. Zwar kennt auch das metaphysische Vorstellen Begriffe. Diese sind jedoch nicht nur hinsichtlich des Grades der Allgemeinheit von den wissenschaftlichen Begriffen unterschieden. Kant hat dies als erster in aller Klarheit gesehen (Kritik der reinen Vernunft, A 843, B 871). Die metaphysischen Begriffe sind im Wesen anderer Art, insofern das, was sie begreifen, und das Begreifen selbst in einem ursprünglichen Sinne das Selbe bleiben. Darum ist es im Bereich der Grundworte des Denkens noch weniger gleichgültig, ob man sie vergißt oder ob man sie unentwegt ungeprüft weitergebracht, vollends dort gebraucht, wo wir aus der Zone heraustreten sollen, in der jene von Ihnen genannten »Be-griffe« das Maßgebende sagen, in der Zone des vollendeten Nihilismus.

Ihre Schrift »Über die Linie« spricht vom Nihilismus als »Grundmacht« (S. 60); sie stellt die Frage nach dem künftigen »Grundwert« (S. 31); sie nennt wiederum die »Gestalt«, »auch die Gestalt des Arbeiters« (S. 41). Diese ist, wenn ich recht sehe, nicht mehr die einzige Gestalt, »darin die Ruhe wohnt« (a. a. O.). Sie sagen vielmehr (S. 10), der Machtbereich des Nihilismus sei von einer Art, daß dort »die fürstliche Erscheinung des Menschen fehlt.« Oder ist die Gestalt des Arbeiters doch jene »neue«, in der sich das fürstliche Erscheinen noch

the knowledge of physical Nature. But just as little can that relation ever be conceived, that is, thought of, without having this conception go back first of all to the transcendental realm of the subject-object relationship. If this has taken place, then only does the question begin as to the origin of the essence of the objectification of being, that is, of the essence of "grasping."

In your and in my case, however, it is a question not even only of concepts of a science, but of basic words, such as, *Gestalt*, dominance, representation, power, will, value, security, of the state of being present (existence) and nothingness which as absence of the state of being present "negates" without ever destroying it. Insofar as nothingness "negates," it confirms itself rather as a distinguished state of being present and veils itself as such. In the basic words named, a kind of language prevails other than scientific assertions. To be sure, metaphysical thinking also knows concepts. These differ, however, from scientific concepts not only in regard to the degree of generality. Kant was the first one to see this in all its clarity (*Critique of Pure Reason*, A 843, B 871). Metaphysical concepts are in their essence of a different sort insofar as that which they comprehend and the comprehension itself remain the same in an original sense. Therefore, in the realm of the basic words of thinking it is even less a matter of indifference whether they are forgotten or whether one keeps on using them untested, and, moreover, uses them there where we should step out of the zone in which the "concepts" named by you say what is authoritative, in the zone of complete nihilism.

Your essay *Across the Line* speaks of nihilism as "fundamental power" (p. 60); it raises the question as to future "fundamental value" (p. 31); it again names the "*Gestalt*," "also the *Gestalt* of the worker" (p. 41). If I see correctly, this is no longer the only *Gestalt* "in which repose dwells" (*Ibid.*). You say rather that the realm of power of nihilism is of such a kind that "the regal appearance of man is lacking" there. Or is the *Gestalt* of the worker, nevertheless, that "new one" in which regal appearance is still

verbirgt? Auch für den Bereich der überquerten Linie kommt es auf die »Sicherheit« an. Auch jetzt bleibt der Schmerz der Prüfstein. Das »Metaphysische« waltet auch im neuen Bereich. Spricht hier das Grundwort »Schmerz« noch aus der gleichen Bedeutung, die Ihre Abhandlung »Über den Schmerz« umgrenzt, in der die Position »des Arbeiters« am weitesten vorgetrieben ist? Behält das Metaphysische auch jenseits der Linie den gleichen Sinn wie im »Arbeiter«, nämlich den des »Gestaltmäßigen?« Oder tritt an die Stelle der Repräsentation der Gestalt eines menschentümlichen Wesens als der vormals einzigen Form der Legitimation des Wirklichen jetzt das »Transzendieren« zu einer »Transzendenz« und Excellenz *nicht*-menschentümlicher sondern göttlicher Art? Kommt das in aller Metaphysik waltende Theologische zum Vorschein? (Über die Linie, S. 32, 39, 41). Wenn Sie in Ihrer Schrift »Das Sanduhrbuch« (1954), S. 106, sagen: »Im Schmerz bewährt sich die Gestalt«, dann behalten Sie, so weit ich sehe, das Grundgefüge Ihres Denkens bei, lassen aber die Grundworte »Schmerz« und »Gestalt« in einem gewandelten, aber noch nicht eigens erläuterten Sinne sprechen. Oder täusche ich mich?

Hier wäre die Stelle, auf Ihre Abhandlung »Über den Schmerz« einzugehen und den inneren Zusammenhang zwischen »Arbeit« und »Schmerz« ans Licht zu heben. Dieser Zusammenhang weist in metaphysische Bezüge, die sich Ihnen von der metaphysischen Position Ihres Werkes »Der Arbeiter« her zeigen. Um die Bezüge, die den Zusammenhang von »Arbeit« und »Schmerz« tragen, deutlicher nachzeichnen zu können, wäre nichts geringeres nötig als den Grundzug der Metaphysik Hegels, die einigende Einheit der »Phänomenologie des Geistes« und der »Wissenschaft der Logik« zu durchdenken. Der Grundzug ist die »absolute Negativität« als die »unendliche Kraft« der Wirklichkeit, d. h. des »existierenden Begriffs«. In der selben (nicht der gleichen) Zugehörigkeit zur Negation der Negation offenbaren Arbeit und Schmerz ihre innerste metaphysische Verwandtschaft. Dieser Hinweis genügt schon, um anzudeuten, welche weitläufigen Erörterungen hier erforderlich wären, um der Sache zu entsprechen. Wagte einer gar die Bezüge zwischen »Arbeit« als dem Grundzug des Seienden und

concealed? Even for the realm of the crossed line it is a question of "security." Even now pain remains the touchstone. The "metaphysical" also pervades in the new realm. Does the basic word "pain" still express here the same meaning which your treatise *Concerning Pain* circumscribes in which the position of *The Worker* is driven furthest forward? Does the metaphysical also retain the same meaning beyond the line as it does in the *Worker,* namely that of "formlike"? Or, in place of the representation of the *Gestalt* of a human essence as the previously unique form of the legitimation of the real, does not "transcending" become a "transcendence" and "Excellency" not of a human but of a divine kind? Is the theological element pervading all metaphysics putting in an appearance? (*Across the Line,* pp. 32, 39, 41). When in your *The Hourglass Book* (1954) p. 106 you say: "In pain *Gestalt* is preserved" then, as far as I can see, you are retaining the basic structure of your thinking but are letting the basic words "pain" and "*Gestalt*" speak in a changed, but not yet expressly elucidated meaning. Or am I mistaken?

This would be the place to enter into a discussion of your treatise *Concerning Pain* and bring to light the inner connection between "work" and "pain." This connection points to metaphysical relations which are apparent to you from the metaphysical position of your work *The Worker.* In order to be able to delineate more clearly the relations which carry the connection between "work" and "pain," nothing less would be necessary than to think through the basic fundamental structure of Hegel's metaphysics, the uniting unity of the *Phenomenology of the Mind* and of the *Science of Logic.* The fundamental character is "absolute negativity" as the "eternal force" of reality, that is, of the "existing concept." In the same (but not the equal) belonging to the negation of the negation, work and pain manifest their innermost metaphysical relationship. This reference already suffices to indicate what extensive discussions would be necessary here in order to do justice to the matter. If anyone would, indeed, dare to think through the relationship between "work" as the basic feature of being and

dem »Schmerz« zurück über Hegels »Logik« durchzudenken, dann käme das griechische Wort für Schmerz, nämlich ἄλγος erst für uns zum Sprechen. Vermutlich ist ἄλγος mit ἀλέγω verwandt, das als Intensivum zu λέγω das innige Versammeln bedeutet. Dann wäre der Schmerz das ins Innigste Versammelnde. Hegels Begriff des »Begriffs« und dessen rechtverstandene »Anstrengung« sagen auf dem gewandelten Boden der absoluten Metaphysik der Subjektivität das Selbe.

Daß Sie auf anderen Wegen in die metaphysischen Bezüge zwischen Arbeit und Schmerz geführt wurden, ist ein schönes Zeugnis dafür, wie Sie in der Weise Ihres metaphysischen Vorstellens auf die Stimme zu hören versuchen, die aus jenen Bezügen vernehmbar wird.

In welcher Sprache spricht der Grundriß des Denkens, das ein Überqueren der Linie vorzeichnet? Soll die Sprache der Metaphysik des Willens zur Macht, der Gestalt und der Werte über die kritische Linie hinübergerettet werden? Wie, wenn gar die Sprache der Metaphysik und die Metaphysik selbst, sei sie die des lebendigen oder toten Gottes, *als* Metaphysik jene Schranke bildeten, die einen Übergang über die Linie, d. h. die Überwindung des Nihilismus verwehrt? Stünde es so, müßte dann das Überqueren der Linie nicht notwendig zu einer Verwandlung des Sagens werden und ein gewandeltes Verhältnis zum Wesen der Sprache verlangen? Und ist nicht Ihr eigener Bezug zur Sprache von einer Art, daß er Ihnen auch eine andere Kennzeichnung der Begriffssprache der Wissenschaften abfordert? Wenn man diese Sprache oft als Nominalismus vorstellt, bleibt man immer noch in die logisch-grammatische Auffassung des Sprachwesens verstrickt.

Ich schreibe dies alles in der Form von Fragen; denn mehr vermag heute, soweit ich sehe, ein Denken nicht, als unablässig das zu bedenken, was die angeführten Fragen hervorruft. Vielleicht kommt der Augenblick, wo das Wesen des Nihilismus auf anderen Wegen sich in einem helleren Lichte deutlicher zeigt. Bis dahin begnüge ich mich mit der Vermutung, wir könnten uns auf das Wesen des Nihilismus nur in der Weise besinnen, daß wir zuvor den Weg einschlagen, der in eine Erörterung des Wesens des Seins führt. Nur auf diesem Weg

"pain" via Hegel's *Logic*, then the Greek word for pain, namely *algos* first becomes articulate for us. Presumably, *algos* is related to *alego* which, as an intensive of *lego* signifies intimate gathering. Then pain would be the most intimate of gatherings. Hegel's concept of the "concept" and its properly understood "tension" say the same thing on the transformed level of the absolute metaphysics of subjectivity.

That you were led in other ways into metaphysical relationships between work and pain is a fine testimony as to how, in the manner of your metaphysical conception, you try to listen to the voice which becomes comprehensible out of those relationships.

In which language does the basic outline of thinking speak which indicates a crossing of the line? Is the language of the metaphysics of the will to power, of *Gestalt,* and of values to be rescued across the critical line? What if even the language of metaphysics and metaphysics itself, whether it be that of the living or of the dead God, *as* metaphysics, formed that barrier which forbids a crossing over of the line, that is, the overcoming of nihilism? If that were the case, would not then the crossing of the line necessarily become a transformation of language and demand a transformed relationship to the essence of language? And is not your own relation to language of a kind that it demands from you a different characterization of the concept-language of the sciences? If this language is often represented as nominalism, then we are still entangled in the logical-grammatical conception of the nature of language.

I am writing all of this in the form of questions; for, as far as I can see, thinking can do no more today than to consider unabatedly what calls forth the above questions. Perhaps the moment will come when the essence of nihilism will be more clearly revealed in other ways in a brighter light. Until then I shall be satisfied with the assumption that we might think of the essence of nihilism only in that way that we first take the path which leads into a discussion of the essence of Being. Only in this way

läßt sich die Frage nach dem Nichts erörtern. *Allein die Frage nach dem Wesen des Seins stirbt ab, wenn sie die Sprache der Metaphysik nicht aufgibt, weil das metaphysische Vorstellen es verwehrt, die Frage nach dem Wesen des Seins zu denken.*

Daß die Verwandlung des Sagens, das dem Wesen des Seins nachdenkt, unter anderen Ansprüchen steht als die Auswechslung einer alten Terminologie gegen eine neue, dürfte einleuchten. Daß ein Bemühen um jene Verwandlung vermutlich noch lange unbeholfen bleibt, ist kein hinreichender Grund, es zu unterlassen. Die Versuchung liegt heute besonders nahe, die Bedachtsamkeit des Denkens nach dem Tempo des Rechnens und Planens abzuschätzen, das seine technischen Erfindungen durch die wirtschaftlichen Erfolge bei jedermann unmittelbar rechtfertigt. Diese Abschätzung des Denkens überfordert es durch Maßstäbe, die ihm fremd sind. Zugleich unterstellt man dem Denken den überheblichen Anspruch, die Lösung der Rätsel zu wissen und das Heil zu bringen. Demgegenüber verdient es die volle Zustimmung, wenn Sie auf die Notwendigkeit hinweisen, alle noch unversehrten Kraftquellen fließen zu lassen und jede Hilfe zur Wirkung zu bringen, um »im Sog des Nihilismus« zu bestehen.

Darüber dürfen wir jedoch die Erörterung des *Wesens* des Nihilismus nicht gering achten, allein schon deshalb nicht, weil dem Nihilismus daran liegt, sein eigenes Wesen zu verstellen und sich dadurch der alles entscheidenden Auseinandersetzung zu entziehen. Erst diese könnte helfen, einen freien Bereich zu öffnen und zu bereiten, worin das erfahren wird, was Sie »eine neue Zuwendung des Seins« nennen (Über die Linie, S. 32).

Sie schreiben: »Der Augenblick, in dem die Linie passiert wird, bringt eine neue Zuwendung des Seins und damit beginnt zu schimmern, was wirklich ist.«

Der Satz ist leicht zu lesen und doch schwer zu denken. Vor allem möchte ich fragen, ob nicht eher umgekehrt die neue Zuwendung des Seins erst den Augenblick für das Passieren der Linie bringe. Die Frage scheint Ihren Satz nur umzukehren. Aber das bloße Umkehren ist jedesmal ein verfängliches Tun. Die Lösung, die es anbieten möchte, bleibt in die Frage ver-

can the question as to nothingness be discussed. *However, the question as to the essence of Being dies off, if it does not surrender the language of metaphysics, because metaphysical conception forbids thinking the question as to the essence of Being.*

That the transformation of the language which contemplates the essence of Being is subject to other demands than the exchanging of an old terminology for a new one, seems to be clear. That an attempt to achieve that transformation presumably will still remain unsuccessful for a long time is not an adequate reason for giving up the attempt. The temptation is especially close at hand today to evaluate the thoughtfulness of thinking according to the tempo of calculating and planning which directly justifies its technical discoveries to everyone through economic successes. This evaluation of thinking asks too much of it by standards which are strange to it. At the same time, thinking is subjected to the presumptuous demand that it know the solution of the riddles and bring salvation. In face of this it deserves full agreement when you point out the necessity of letting all still untapped springs of power flow and of bringing every aid to bear in order to hold one's own "in the wake of nihilism."

In doing so we must, however, not hold lightly the discussion of the *essence* of nihilism, already for the reason alone that nihilism is concerned with disguising its own essence and thereby withdrawing from the all-deciding discussion. Only this might help to open up and prepare a free area in which that will be experienced which you call "a new" direction of Being (*Across the Line,* p. 32).

You write: "The moment in which the line is crossed brings a new direction of Being and with it there begins to shimmer what is real."

The sentence is easy to read but difficult to think. Above all I should like to ask whether, on the contrary, it is not rather the new direction of Being which first brings the moment for the crossing of the line. The question seems only to reverse your sentence. But mere reversal is each time a risky procedure. The solution which it might offer remains involved in the question

strickt, die sie umgekehrt hat. Ihr Satz sagt, das, »was wirklich ist«, also das Wirkliche, d. h. das Seiende beginnt zu schimmern, weil das Sein sich neu zuwendet. Darum fragen wir jetzt gemäßer, ob »das Sein« etwas für sich ist und ob es außerdem und bisweilen auch sich den Menschen zuwendet. Vermutlich ist die Zuwendung selber, aber noch verhülltcr-weise, Jenes, was wir verlegen genug und unbestimmt »das Sein« nennen. Allein geschieht solche Zuwendung nicht auch noch und in einer seltsamen Weise unter der Herrschaft des Nihilismus, nämlich in der Weise, daß »das Sein« sich abwendet und sich in die Absenz entzieht? Abwendung und Entzug sind jedoch nicht nichts. Sie walten fast bedrängender für den Menschen, sodaß sie ihn fortziehen, sein Trachten und Tun ansaugen und es schließlich so in den sich entziehenden Sog aufsaugen, daß der Mensch meinen kann, er begegne nur noch sich selbst. In Wahrheit ist jedoch sein Selbst nichts anderes mehr als der Verbrauch seiner Ek-sistenz in die Herrschaft dessen, was Sie als den totalen Arbeitscharakter kennzeichnen.

Freilich lassen Zuwendung und Abwendung des Seins, wenn wir genügend auf sie achten, sich nie vorstellen, gleich als ob sie nur dann und wann und für Augenblicke auf den Menschen träfen. Das Menschenwesen beruht vielmehr darauf, daß es jeweils so oder so in der Zuwendung und Abwendung währt und wohnt. Wir sagen vom »Sein selbst« immer *zuwenig*, wenn wir, »das Sein« sagend, das An-wesen *zum* Menschen*wesen* auslassen und dadurch verkennen, daß dieses Wesen selbst »das Sein« mitausmacht. Wir sagen auch vom Menschen immer *zuwenig*, wenn wir, das »Sein« (nicht das Menschsein) sagend, den Menschen für sich setzen und das so Gesetzte dann erst noch in eine Beziehung zum »Sein« bringen. Wir sagen aber auch *zuviel*, wenn wir das Sein als das Allumfassende meinen und dabei den Menschen nur als ein besonderes Seiendes unter anderen (Pflanze, Tier) vorstellen und beides in die Beziehung setzen; denn schon im Menschenwesen liegt die Beziehung zu dem, was durch den Bezug, das Beziehen im Sinne des Brauchens, als »Sein« bestimmt und so seinem vermeintlichen »an und für sich« entnommen ist. Die Rede vom »Sein« jagt das Vorstellen von

which has reversed it. Your sentence says that "which is real," in other words, the real, which means that being begins to shimmer because Being takes a new direction. Therefore, we now ask more properly whether "Being" is something for itself and whether it also and at times turns in the direction of man. Presumably the turning itself, but still obscurely, is that which we embarrassedly enough, and vaguely call "Being." But does such turning-toward not also take place and, in a strange manner, under the dominance of nihilism, namely in such a way that "Being" turns away and withdraws into the state of absence? Turning away and withdrawal are, however, not nothing. They prevail perhaps even more urgently for man so that they pull him along, suck themselves fast to his thoughts and actions and, finally, suck them into the withdrawing wake in such a way that man can believe that he is only encountering himself. In truth, however, his self is no longer anything more than the using of his human reality into the dominance of what you characterize as the total character of work.

To be sure, the turning towards and away of Being, if we pay sufficient attention to them, never present themselves, just as if they touched man only occasionally and only momentarily. The essence of man rather depends on the fact that it endures and dwells for a time in either the turning towards or away. We always say *too little* of "Being itself" when in saying "Being," we leave out the being present *in* the essence of man and thereby fail to recognize that this essence itself helps to determine "Being." We also always say *too little* of man if, in saying "Being" (not being human), we set man apart and then only bring that which has thus been set apart into relationship with "Being." We also say *too much*, however, if we mean Being as the all-encompassing and thereby represent man only as a special being among others (plants, animals) and put both into the relationship; for there already lies in the essence of man the relationship to that which through the relation determines the relating as "Being" in the sense of using and it is thus deprived of its presumable "in and for itself." The talk of "Being" drives the conception from

einer Verlegenheit in die andere, ohne daß sich die Quelle dieser Ratlosigkeit zeigen möchte.

Doch alles kommt, so scheint es, sogleich in die beste Ordnung, wenn wir längst Gedachtes nicht geflissentlich außerachtlassen: die Subjekt-Objekt-Beziehung. Sie sagt, zu jedem Subjekt (Mensch) gehöre ein Objekt (Sein) und umgekehrt. Gewiß; wenn nur nicht dieses Ganze – die Beziehung, das Subjekt, das Objekt – schon im Wesen dessen beruhte, was wir, wie sich zeigte, ganz unzureichend als Beziehung zwischen Sein und Mensch vorstellen. Subjektivität und Objektivität gründen ihrerseits schon in einer eigentümlichen Offenbarkeit des »Seins« und des »Menschenwesens«. Sie legt das Vorstellen auf die Unterscheidung beider als Objekt und Subjekt fest. Diese gilt seitdem als absolut und bannt das Denken ins Ausweglose. Eine Ansetzung des »Seins«, die »das Sein« aus der Rücksicht auf die Subjekt-Objekt-Beziehung nennen möchte, bedenkt nicht, was sie schon an Fragwürdigem ungedacht läßt. So bleibt denn die Rede von einer »Zuwendung des Seins« ein Notbehelf und durchaus fragwürdig, weil das Sein in der Zuwendung beruht, sodaß diese nie erst zum »Sein« hinzutreten kann.

Anwesen (»Sein«) ist als Anwesen je und je Anwesen zum Menschenwesen, insofern Anwesen Geheiß ist, das jeweils das Menschenwesen ruft. Das Menschenwesen ist als solches hörend, weil es ins rufende Geheiß, ins An-wesen gehört. Dieses jedes Mal Selbe, das Zusammengehören von Ruf und Gehör, wäre dann »das Sein«? Was sage ich? »Sein« ist es durchaus nicht mehr, – wenn wir »Sein«, wie es geschicklich waltet, nämlich als Anwesen, voll auszudenken versuchen, auf welche Weise allein wir seinem geschicklichen Wesen entsprechen. Dann müßten wir das vereinzelnde und trennende Wort: »das Sein« ebenso entschieden fahren lassen wie den Namen: »der Mensch«. Die Frage nach der Beziehung beider enthüllte sich als unzureichend, weil sie niemals in den Bereich dessen gelangt, was sie erfragen möchte. In Wahrheit können wir dann nicht einmal mehr sagen, »das Sein« und »der Mensch« »seien« das Selbe in dem Sinne, daß *sie* zusammengehören; denn *so* sagend, lassen wir immer noch beide für sich sein.

one embarrassment into another without revealing the source of this perplexity.

But, everything is at once in good order, so it seems, if we do not purposely disregard what has long since been thought of: the subject-object relationship. This means that to every subject (man) belongs an object (Being) and vice versa. Certainly; if only this totality—the relationship, the subject, the object—did not already rest in the essence of that which, quite inadequately, as has been shown, we represent as the relationship between Being and man. Subjectivity and objectivity for their part already have their basis in a peculiar manifestation of "Being" and the "essence of man." It establishes the conception on the level of differentiation of both as object and subject. This has since then been regarded as absolute and makes it impossible for thinking to find a way out. A determination of "Being" which would like to name "Being" out of consideration for the subject-object relationship, does not consider those matters it already leaves unthought of in that which is worthy of being questioned. Thus the talk of a "turning-towards on the part of Being" is a makeshift and completely questionable because Being depends on the turning-towards so that this turning can never approach "Being" first.

Being present ("Being") as being present always is a being present for the essence of man, insofar as being present is a demand which at times summons the essence of man. The essence of man as such is in a state of hearing because it belongs in the summoning demand, belongs in its being present.[2] This belonging together of summoning and hearing, which is always the same, could that be "Being"? What am I saying? It is no longer "Being" at all if we try to think fully and completely of "Being" as it is fated to hold sway, namely as being present, in which way alone we refer to its destined essence. Then we should just as decidedly have to drop the singularizing and separating word "Being" as to drop the name "man." The question as to the relationship of both revealed itself as inadequate because it never reaches into the realm of what it would like to question. In truth, we can then not even say any longer that "Being" and "man" "be" the same in the sense that *they* belong together; for in *so* saying we still let both be for themselves.

[2] Being present reveals a being in relation to essence.

Doch wozu erwähne ich in einem Brief über das Wesen des vollendeten Nihilismus diese umständlichen und abstrakten Sachen? Einmal um anzudeuten, daß es keineswegs leichter ist, »das Sein« zu sagen, als vom Nichts zu sprechen; sodann aber, um erneut zu zeigen, wie unabwendbar hier alles auf das rechte Sagen ankommt, auf jenen *Λόγος*, dessen Wesen die aus der Metaphysik stammende Logik und Dialektik nie zu erfahren vermag.

Liegt es am »Sein« – das Wort nenne jetzt für einen Augenblick jenes fragwürdige Selbe, worin das Wesen des Seins und das Wesen des Menschen zusammengehören – liegt es am »Sein«, daß in der Entsprechung zu ihm unser Sagen versagt und nur das bleibt, was man durch die Betitelung »Mystik« allzu eilig verdächtigt? Oder liegt es an unserem Sagen, daß es noch nicht spricht, weil es sich noch nicht in eine Entsprechung zum Wesen des »Seins« zu schicken vermag? Ist es dem Belieben der Sagenden überlassen, welche Sprache der Grundworte sie im Augenblick des Überquerens der Linie, d. h. beim Durchqueren der kritischen Zone des vollendeten Nihilismus sprechen? Genügt es, wenn diese Sprache allgemein verständlich ist, oder walten hier andere Gesetze und Maße, die ebenso einzigartig sind wie der weltgeschichtliche Augenblick der planetarischen Vollendung des Nihilismus und die Aus-einander-setzung seines Wesens?

Das sind Fragen, die kaum erst beginnen, uns so fragwürdig zu werden, daß wir uns in ihnen heimisch finden und nicht mehr von ihnen lassen, selbst auf die Gefahr, alteingesessene Gewöhnungen des Denkens im Sinne des metaphysischen Vorstellens preisgeben zu müssen und der Mißachtung aller gesunden Vernunft geziehen zu werden.

Das sind Fragen, die beim Gang »über die Linie« noch eine besondere Schärfe bekunden; denn dieser Gang bewegt sich im Bereich des Nichts. Verschwindet mit der Vollendung oder wenigstens mit der Überwindung des Nihilismus das Nichts? Vermutlich kommt es erst dann zu dieser Überwindung, wenn statt des Anscheins des nichtigen Nichts das einsther ins »Sein« verwandte Wesen des Nichts ankommen und bei uns Sterblichen unterkommen kann.

But why am I mentioning these involved and abstract matters in a letter about the essence of complete nihilism? First of all, in order to indicate that it is by no means easier to say "Being" than to speak of nothingness; but also, in order to show once more, how inevitably everything depends here on the proper wording, on that *Logos* whose essence logic and dialectics, which stem from metaphysics, are never able to experience.

Is it the fault of "Being"—may that word for the moment designate that questionable sameness in which the essence of Being and the essence of man belong together—is it the fault of "Being" that our words fail in referring to it and only that remains on which suspicion is cast all too hastily as "mysticism"? Or is our language at fault for not yet speaking because it is not yet able to adapt itself to a reference to the essence of "Being"? Is it left to the arbitrariness of those who speak, which language of basic words they are going to speak at the moment of crossing over the line, that is, in traversing the critical zone of complete nihilism? Is it sufficient if this language is generally comprehensible or do other laws and standards prevail here which are just as unique as the world-historical moment of the planetary completion of nihilism and the discussion of its essence?

These are questions which no sooner begin to become worthy of question than we find ourselves at home in them and do not give them up any more, even at the risk of having to abandon old established habits of thinking in the sense of metaphysical conceptions and of being accused of disdain for all sound reason.

These are questions which exhibit a special sharpness while passing "across the line," for this passage moves in the realm of nothingness. Does nothingness vanish with the completion, or at least with the overcoming of nihilism? Presumably, overcoming is only attained when, instead of the appearance of negative nothingness, the essence of nothingness which was once related to "Being" can arrive and be accepted by us mortals.

Woher kommt dieses Wesen? Wo haben wir es zu suchen? Welches ist der Ort des Nichts? Wir fragen nicht unbedacht zuviel, wenn wir nach dem Ort suchen und das Wesen der Linie erörtern. Doch ist dies etwas anderes als der Versuch, das zu leisten, was Sie verlangen: »eine gute Definition des Nihilismus«? Es sieht so aus, als werde das Denken wie in einem magischen Kreis fortgesetzt um das Selbe herumgeführt oder gar herumgenarrt, ohne sich doch je diesem Selben nähern zu können. Aber vielleicht ist der Kreis eine verborgene Spirale. Vielleicht hat sich diese inzwischen verengt. Dies bedeutet: die Art und die Weise, nach denen wir uns dem Wesen des Nihilismus nähern, wandeln sich. Die Güte der rechtmäßig verlangten »guten Definition« findet ihre Bewährung darin, daß wir das Definierenwollen aufgeben, insofern dieses sich auf Aussagesätze festlegen muß, in denen das Denken abstirbt. Doch bleibt es ein geringer, weil ein nur negativer Gewinn, wenn wir darauf achten lernen, daß sich über das Nichts und das Sein und den Nihilismus, über deren Wesen und über das Wesen (verbal) des Wesens (nominal) keine Auskunft erteilen läßt, die in der Form von Aussagesätzen griffbereit vorliegen kann.

Es bleibt insofern ein Gewinn, als wir erfahren, daß jenes, dem die »gute Definition« gelten soll, das Wesen des Nihilismus, uns in einen Bereich verweist, der ein anderes Sagen verlangt. Gehört zum »Sein« die Zuwendung und zwar so, daß jenes in dieser beruht, dann löst sich das »Sein« in die Zuwendung auf. Diese wird jetzt das Fragwürdige, als welches fortan das Sein bedacht wird, das in sein Wesen zurück und darin aufgegangen ist. Dementsprechend kann der denkende Vorblick in diesen Bereich das »Sein« nur noch in folgender Weise schreiben: das ~~Sein~~. Die kreuzweise Durchstreichung wehrt zunächst nur ab, nämlich die fast unausrottbare Gewöhnung, »das Sein« wie ein für sich stehendes und dann auf den Menschen erst bisweilen zukommendes Gegenüber vorzustellen. Dieser Vorstellung gemäß hat es dann den Anschein, als sei der Mensch vom »Sein« ausgenommen. Indes ist er nicht nur nicht ausgenommen, d. h. nicht nur ins »Sein« einbegriffen, sondern »Sein« ist, das Menschenwesen brauchend, darauf an-

Where does this essence come from? Where do we have to look for it? What is the place of nothingness? We do not thoughtlessly ask too much when we look for the place and discuss the essence of the line. But is this any different from the attempt to achieve what you ask for, "a good definition of nihilism"? It looks as if thinking were continually being led, or driven like a fool, as though in a magic circle around the Sameness without ever being able to approach this Sameness. But perhaps the circle is a hidden spiral. Perhaps it has narrowed in the interim. This means that the ways in which we are approaching the essence of nihilism are changing. The "goodness" of the rightfully demanded "good definition" finds its confirmation in our giving up the wish to define in so far as this must be established on assertions in which thinking dies out. However, it is a gain, which is slight because it is only negative, if we learn to notice that no information can be given about nothingness and Being and nihilism, about their essence and about the essence (verbal) of the essence (nominal) which can be presented tangibly in the form of assertions.

It is a gain insofar as we learn that that to which the "good definition" is to apply, the essence of nihilism, leads us into a realm which requires a different language. If turning-towards belongs to "Being" and in such a way that the latter is based on the former, then "Being" is dissolved in this turning. It now becomes questionable what Being which has reverted into and been absorbed by its essence is henceforth to be thought of. Accordingly, a thoughtful glance ahead into this realm of "Being" can only write it as ~~Being~~. The drawing of these crossed lines at first only repels, especially the almost ineradicable habit of conceiving "Being" as something standing by itself and only coming at times face to face with man. According to this conception it looks as if man were excluded from "Being." However, he is not only not excluded, that is, he is not only encompassed into "Being" but "Being," using the essence of man, is obliged to abandon

gewiesen, den Anschein des Für-sich preiszugeben, weshalb es auch anderen Wesens ist, als die Vorstellung eines Inbegriffes wahrhaben möchte, der die Subjekt-Objekt-Beziehung umgreift.

Das Zeichen der Durchkreuzung kann nach dem Gesagten allerdings kein bloß negatives Zeichen der Durchstreichung sein. Es zeigt vielmehr in die vier Gegenden des Gevierts und deren Versammlung im Ort der Durchkreuzung (vgl. Vorträge und Aufsätze, 1954, S. 145–204).

Das An-wesen wendet sich als solches zum Menschenwesen, worin sich die Zuwendung erst vollendet, insofern jenes, das Menschenwesen, ihrer gedenkt. Der Mensch ist in seinem Wesen das Gedächtnis des Seins, aber des ~~Seins~~. Dies sagt: das Menschenwesen gehört mit zu dem, was in der kreuzweisen Durchstreichung des Seins das Denken in den Anspruch eines anfänglicheren Geheißes nimmt. An-wesen gründet in der Zuwendung, die als solche das Menschenwesen in sie verwendet, daß es für sie sich verschwende.

Wie das ~~Sein~~, so müßte auch das Nichts geschrieben und d. h. gedacht werden. Darin liegt: zum Nichts gehört, nicht als Zugabe nur, das gedenkende Menschenwesen. Wenn daher im Nihilismus das Nichts auf eine besondere Weise zur Herrschaft gelangt, dann ist der Mensch nicht nur vom Nihilismus betroffen, sondern wesenhaft an ihm beteiligt. Dann steht aber auch der ganze menschliche »Bestand« nicht irgendwo diesseits der Linie, um sie zu überqueren und jenseits ihrer sich beim Sein anzusiedeln. Das Menschenwesen gehört selber zum Wesen des Nihilismus und somit zur Phase seiner Vollendung. Der Mensch macht als jenes in das ~~Sein~~ gebrauchte Wesen die Zone des ~~Seins~~ und d. h. zugleich des Nichts mit aus. Der Mensch steht nicht nur *in* der kritischen Zone der Linie. Er *ist* selbst, aber nicht er für sich und vollends nicht durch sich allein, diese Zone und somit die Linie. In keinem Falle ist die Linie, als Zeichen der Zone des vollendeten Nihilismus gedacht, solches, was wie ein Überschreitbares vor dem Menschen liegt. Dann fällt aber auch die Möglichkeit eines trans lineam und ihres Überquerens dahin.

Je mehr wir über »die Linie« nachdenken, um so mehr verschwindet dieses unmittelbar eingängige Bild, ohne daß die

the appearance of the for-itself, for which reason, it is also of a different nature than the conception of totality would like to have it, which encompasses the subject-object relationship.

The symbol of crossed lines can, to be sure, according to what has been said, not be a merely negative symbol of crossing out. Rather it points into the four areas of the quadrangle and of their gathering at the point of intersection (cf. *Vorträge und Aufsätze*, 1954, pp. 145-204). The being present as such turns towards the essence of man in which the turning-towards is first completed, insofar as the human being remembers it. Man in his essence is the memory of Being, but of ~~Being~~. This means that the essence of man is a part of that which in the crossed intersected lines of Being puts thinking under the claim of an earlier demand. Being present is grounded in the turning-towards which as such turns the essence of man into it so that the latter may dissipate itself for it.

Nothingness would have to be written, and that means thought of, just like ~~Being~~. Inherent in this is that the essence of man which remembers belongs to nothingness and not only as something added. If, therefore, in nihilism nothingness attains dominance in a special manner, then man is not only affected by nihilism but has an essential share in it. But then the entire human "component realities" also do not stand somewhere on this side of the line in order to cross over it and to settle down on the other side next to Being. The essence of man itself belongs to the essence of nihilism and thereby to the phase of its completion. Man, as the essence put into use in ~~Being~~ helps to constitute the zone of ~~Being~~ and that means at the same time of nothingness. Man does not only stand *in* the critical zone of the line. He himself, but not he for himself and particularly not through himself alone, *is* this zone and thus the line. In no case is the line, thought of as a symbol of the zone of complete nihilism, like something impassable lying before man. Then the possibility of a *trans lineam* and its crossing also vanishes.

The more we think about "the line," the more does this directly accessible picture vanish without making it necessary for the

Gedanken, die sich an ihm entzünden, ihre Bedeutung verlieren müssen. In der Schrift »Über die Linie« geben Sie eine Ortsbeschreibung des Nihilismus und eine Beurteilung der Lage und der Bewegungsmöglichkeit des Menschen im Hinblick auf den beschriebenen, durch das Bild der Linie bezeichneten Ort. Gewiß bedarf es einer Topographie des Nihilismus, seines Vorganges und seiner Überwindung. Aber der Topographie muß eine Topologie voraufgehen: die Erörterung desjenigen Ortes, der Sein und Nichts in ihr Wesen versammelt, das Wesen des Nihilismus bestimmt und so die Wege erkennen läßt, auf denen sich die Weisen einer möglichen Überwindung des Nihilismus abzeichnen.

Wohin gehören Sein und Nichts, zwischen denen spielend der Nihilismus sein Wesen entfaltet? In der Schrift »Über die Linie« (S. 22 ff.) nennen Sie als ein Hauptkennzeichen der nihilistischen Strömungen »die Reduktion«: »Der Überfluß versiegt: der Mensch empfindet sich als Ausgebeuteter in mannigfachen und nicht nur ökonomischen Beziehungen.« Sie fügen aber mit Recht hinzu: »das schließt nicht aus, daß sie (die Reduktion) auf weite Strecken mit wachsender Machtentfaltung und Durchschlagskraft verbunden ist«, wie denn auch der Schwund »ja nicht lediglich Schwund ist« (S. 23).

Was sagt dies anderes als: die Bewegung zum Immerweniger an Fülle und an Ursprünglichem innerhalb des Seienden im Ganzen wird durch ein Anwachsen des Willens zur Macht nicht nur begleitet sondern bestimmt. Der Wille zur Macht ist der Wille, der *sich* will. Als dieser Wille und in dessen Ordnungen erscheint, früh vorgebildet und in vielerlei Weisen waltend, jenes, was vom Seienden her vorgestellt, dieses übersteigt und innerhalb des Übersteigs auf das Seiende zurückwirkt, sei es als der Grund des Seienden, sei es als dessen Verursachung. Die innerhalb des Seienden feststellbare Reduktion beruht auf einer Produktion des Seins, nämlich auf der Entfaltung des Willens zur Macht in den unbedingten Willen zum Willen. Der Schwund, die Absenz, ist aus einer Praesenz her und durch diese bestimmt. Sie geht allem Schwindenden vorauf, übersteigt es. So waltet denn auch dort, wo das Seiende hinschwindet, nicht nur dieses für sich, sondern in maßgebender Weise

thoughts which are enkindled by it to lose their meaning. In the article *Across the Line* you give a description of the location of nihilism and an estimation of the situation and of the possibility of man's movement in respect to the place described and designated by the picture of the line. A topography of nihilism, of its process, and of its overcoming is certainly needed. But the topography must be preceded by a topology: the discussion of that place which gathers Being and nothingness into its essence, determines the essence of nihilism, and thus makes known the paths on which the ways of a possible overcoming of nihilism are indicated.

Where do Being and nothingness belong between which nihilism easily unfolds its essence? In the article *Across the Line* (pp. 22ff.) you name "reduction" as a main characteristic of nihilistic currents: 'The surplus is exhausted; man feels that he is exploited in many, not only economic, respects." You are right in adding: "that does not exclude the fact that it (reduction) is connected in wide areas with a growing development of force and striking power," just as cessation "is, of course, not merely cessation" (p. 23).

What else does this say other than that the movement of diminishing returns of abundance and of what is original within the being in totality is not only accompanied but is determined by a growth of the will to power. The will to power is the will that wills *itself*. As this will, and in its structures, there appears, pre-formed at an early stage and prevailing in manifold ways, that which, represented as coming from being, climbs past it and within this climb has a backward effect on being, whether it be as the basis of being or as its cause. The reduction determinable within being is based on a production of Being, namely on the unfolding of the will to power into the unconditioned will to will. Disappearance, absence, is determined from out of a state of presence and through it. It precedes everything which disappears, rises above it. Thus, also there whither being vanishes, not only the latter prevails for itself but something else does so previously in a decisive way. Everywhere the rising

zuvor ein Anderes. Überall ist der auf das Seiende zurückkommende Überstieg, das »transcendens schlechthin« (Sein und Zeit, § 7), »das Sein« des Seienden. Überstieg ist die Metaphysik selbst, wobei dieser Name jetzt nicht eine Lehre und Disciplin der Philosophie meint, sondern dieses, daß »es« jenen Überstieg »gibt« (Sein und Zeit, § 43c). Er ist gegeben, insofern er auf den Weg seines Waltens gebracht, d. h. geschickt ist. Die unberechenbare Fülle und Jähe dessen, was sich als Überstieg entfaltet, heißt das Geschick der (Gen. object.) Metaphysik.

Diesem Geschick gemäß wird das menschliche Vorstellen selbst ein metaphysisches. Die metaphysischen Vorstellungen vom Seienden lassen sich zwar historisch in ihrer Abfolge als ein Geschehen darstellen. Aber dieses Geschehen ist nicht die Geschichte des Seins, sondern dieses waltet als das Geschick des Überstiegs. Daß und wie »es« das Sein des Seienden »gibt«, ist die Meta-Physik in dem bezeichneten Sinne.

Das Nichts gehört, auch wenn wir es nur im Sinne des völligen Nicht von Anwesendem meinen, ab-wesend zum Anwesen als eine von dessen Möglichkeiten. Wenn somit im Nihilismus das Nichts waltet und das Wesen des Nichts zum Sein gehört, das Sein jedoch das Geschick des Überstiegs ist, dann zeigt sich als Wesensort des Nihilismus das Wesen der Metaphysik. Dies läßt sich nur dann und solange sagen, als wir das Wesen der Metaphysik als das Geschick des Überstiegs erfahren.

Worin beruht dann die Überwindung des Nihilismus? In der Verwindung der Metaphysik. Das ist ein anstößiger Gedanke. Man versucht, ihm auszuweichen. Um so weniger besteht ein Anlaß, ihn abzumildern. Doch wird die Aufnahme jenes Gedankens auf geringeren Widerstand treffen, wenn wir beachten, daß ihm zufolge das Wesen des Nihilismus nichts Nihilistisches ist und der alten Würde der Metaphysik dadurch nichts genommen wird, wenn ihr eigenes Wesen den Nihilismus in sich birgt.

Die Zone der kritischen Linie, d. h. die Ortschaft des Wesens des vollendeten Nihilismus wäre sonach dort zu suchen, wo das Wesen der Metaphysik seine äußersten Möglichkeiten entfaltet und sich in sie zusammennimmt. Das geschieht dort,

above which comes back to being, "transcendence per se" (*Sein und Zeit,* § 7), is "the Being" of being. Transcendence is metaphysics itself, whereby this name now does not signify a doctrine and discipline of philosophy but signifies that "it" "gives" that transcendence (*Sein und Zeit,* § 43c). It is given in so far as it is brought, that is, sent, on the path of its prevailing. The incalculable abundance and suddenness of that which unfolds as transcendence is called the fate of (Gen. object.) metaphysics.

According to this fate, human conception itself becomes metaphysical. The metaphysical conceptions of being can, to be sure, be represented historically in their sequence as an event. But this event is not the history of Being but, on the contrary, the latter prevails as the fate of transcendence. That and how "it" "gives" the Being of being is meta-physics in the indicated sense.

Nothingness, even when we mean it only in the sense of the complete negative of what is present, in being absent, belongs to being present as one of its possibilities. If, therefore, nothingness prevails in nihilism and the essence of nothingness belongs to Being, although Being is the fate of transcendence, then the essence of metaphysics is shown to be the place of the essence of nihilism. This can be said only and as long as we experience the essence of metaphysics as the fate of transcendence.

On what is the overcoming of nihilism based? On the restoration of metaphysics. That is a repelling thought. We try to evade it. So much less is there any reason to soften it. Nevertheless, the acceptance of that idea will meet with less resistance if we note that in consequence of it the essence of nihilism is nothing nihilistic and through it nothing is taken from the old dignity of metaphysics if its own essence contains nihilism in it.

The zone of the critical line, that is, the locale of the essence of complete nihilism, would accordingly have to be sought where the essence of metaphysics unfolds its utmost possibilities and gathers itself together in them. That takes place where the will

wo der Wille zum Willen alles Anwesende einzig nur in der durchgängigen und einförmigen Bestellbarkeit seines Bestandes will, d. h. herausfordert, *stellt.* Als die unbedingte Versammlung solchen Stellens schwindet das ~~Sein~~ nicht hin. Es bricht in einer einzigen Unheimlichkeit auf. Im Schwund und in der Reduktion zeigt sich nur das vormals Anwesende, das der Wille zum Willen noch nicht ergriffen, sondern noch im Willen des Geistes und dessen totaler Selbstbewegung belassen hat, in der Hegels Denken sich bewegt.

Der Schwund des vormals Anwesenden ist kein Verschwinden des Anwesens. Wohl dagegen entzieht sich dieses. Indes bleibt der Entzug dem nihilistisch bestimmten Vorstellen verborgen. Es hat den Anschein, als genüge das Anwesende im Sinne des Bestandes sich selbst. Dessen Beständigkeit und das, was in solche Ständigkeit stellt, das An-wesen des Anwesenden, erscheinen, wenn die Rede darauf kommt, als eine Erfindung des schweifenden Denkens, das vor lauter »Sein« das Seiende, die vermeintlich einzige »Wirklichkeit«, nicht mehr zu sehen vermag.

In der Phase des vollendeten Nihilismus sieht es so aus, als gäbe es dergleichen wie *Sein des* Seienden nicht, als sei es mit dem Sein nichts (im Sinne des nichtigen Nichts). ~~Sein~~ bleibt in einer seltsamen Weise aus. Es verbirgt sich. Es hält sich in einer Verborgenheit, die sich selber verbirgt. In solchem Verbergen beruht jedoch das griechisch erfahrene Wesen der Vergessenheit. Sie ist am Ende, d. h. aus dem Beginn ihres Wesens her nichts Negatives, sondern als Ver-bergung vermutlich ein Bergen, das noch Unentborgenes verwahrt. Für das geläufige Vorstellen gerät das Vergessen leicht in den Anschein des bloßen Versäumens, des Mangels und des Mißlichen. Nach der Gewohnheit nehmen wir Vergessen und Vergeßlichkeit ausschließlich als eine Unterlassung, die man häufig genug als einen Zustand des für sich vorgestellten Menschen antreffen kann. Von einer Bestimmung des Wesens der Vergessenheit bleiben wir noch weit entfernt. Doch wir geraten selbst dort, wo wir das Wesen der Vergessenheit in seiner Weite erblickt haben, allzu leicht in die Gefahr, das Vergessen nur als menschliches Tun und Lassen zu verstehen.

to will wills, that is, challenges, *places* everything present solely in the general and uniform placeability of its component parts. As the unconditioned gathering together of such placement ~~Being~~ does not disappear. It moves off in an unique estrangement. In the disappearance and in the reduction is shown only what was once present which the will to will has not yet grasped but has still left in the will of the spirit and its total self-movement, in which Hegel's thinking moves.

The disappearance of what has once been present is no vanishing of the present. On the contrary, the latter does, indeed, withdraw. However, the withdrawal remains hidden from the nihilistically determined conception. It seems as if what is present, in the sense of the component realities, is sufficient unto itself. Its state of stability and that which places it in such a state, the being present of what is present, appear, when they are mentioned, as an invention of unstable thinking which no longer is able to see being, which is presumably the only "reality," because of so much "Being."

In the phase of complete nihilism it looks as if there were no such thing as *Being of* being, as though there were no such thing as Being (in the sense of negative nothingness). ~~Being~~ is left out in a strange way. It conceals itself. It remains in a concealment which also conceals itself. In such concealing there is based, however, the essence of oblivion known to the Greeks. It is at the end, that is, from the beginning of its essence nothing negative, but as a concealment presumably a sheltering which still preserves what has not yet been revealed. For the ordinary conception, forgetting easily takes on the appearance of mere neglect, of a lack, of something disagreeable. Through habit we take forgetting and forgetfulness exclusively as an omission, which can be encountered frequently enough as a state of the man conceived of as himself. We are still far distant from a determination of the essence of oblivion. But even where we have caught sight of the essence of oblivion in its extensiveness we far too easily run the risk of understanding forgetting only as human commission and omission.

Die »Seinsvergessenheit« hat man denn auch vielfach so vorgestellt, daß, um es im Bilde zu sagen, das Sein der Schirm ist,
den die Vergeßlichkeit eines Philosophieprofessors irgendwo
hat stehen lassen.

Indessen *befällt* die Vergessenheit als anscheinend von ihm
Getrenntes nicht nur das Wesen des Seins. Sie gehört zur
Sache des Seins selbst, waltet als Geschick seines Wesens. Die
recht bedachte Vergessenheit, die Verbergung des noch unent-
borgenen Wesens (verbal) des ~~Seins~~, birgt ungehobene Schätze
und ist das Versprechen eines Fundes, der nur auf das gemäße
Suchen wartet. Um solches zu vermuten, bedarf es keiner prophetischen Gabe und nicht der Manier von Verkündern, sondern nur der jahrzehntelang geübten Achtung des Gewesenen,
das sich im metaphysischen Denken des Abendlandes bekundet.
Dieses Gewesene steht im Zeichen der Unverborgenheit des
Anwesenden. Die Unverborgenheit beruht in der Verborgenheit des Anwesens. *Dieser* Verborgenheit, in der die Unverborgenheit (᾿Αλήϑεια) gründet, gilt das Andenken. Es denkt
jenes Gewesende an, das nicht vergangen ist, weil es das Un-
vergängliche in allem Währen bleibt, das je das Ereignis des
~~Seins~~ gewährt.

Die Verwindung der Metaphysik ist Verwindung der Seinsvergessenheit. Die Verwindung wendet sich dem Wesen der
Metaphysik zu. Sie umrankt es durch das, wohin dieses Wesen
selbst verlangt, insofern es nach demjenigen Bereich ruft, der
es ins Freie seiner Wahrheit hebt. Darum muß das Denken,
um der Verwindung der Metaphysik zu entsprechen, zuvor das
Wesen der Metaphysik verdeutlichen. Einem solchen Versuch
erscheint die Verwindung der Metaphysik zunächst wie eine
Überwindung, die das ausschließlich metaphysische Vorstellen
nur hinter sich bringt, um das Denken ins Freie des verwunde-
nen Wesens der Metaphysik zu geleiten. Aber in der Verwindung kehrt die bleibende Wahrheit der anscheinend verstoßen-
nen Metaphysik als deren nunmehr angeeignetes *Wesen* erst
eigens zurück.

Hier geschieht anderes als eine bloße Restauration der Metaphysik. Überdies gibt es auch keine Restauration, die das
Überlieferte nur so aufnehmen könnte, wie einer die vom

"Oblivion of Being" has frequently been so represented that, to put it graphically, Being is an umbrella which the forgetfulness of a professor of philosophy has left somewhere.

However, oblivion, as something apparently separated from it, does not *affect* only the essence of Being. It is an affair of Being itself, governs the fate of its essence. Properly considered oblivion, the concealment of the still unrevealed being (verbal) of ~~Being~~ preserves untouched treasures and is the promise of a find which is only waiting for the proper search. In order to assume something of this sort, no prophetic gift is required and not the affectation of soothsayers, but only the decade-long attention paid to what has been, as evidenced in the metaphysical thinking of the West. This past is signalized by the unconcealedness of what is present. Unconcealedness is based on the concealment of the present. Remembrance applies to *this* concealment in which unconcealedness (*Alitheia*) is based. It thinks back to that which has been, which has not disappeared because it remains what is imperishable in all that is lasting which the event of ~~Being~~ ever grants.

The restoration of metaphysics is the restoration of the oblivion of Being. This restoration turns towards the essence of metaphysics. It entwines itself around it through that towards which this essence itself yearns, insofar as it summons that zone which lifts it into the freedom of its truth. For that reason, thinking, in order to refer to the restoration of metaphysics, must first clarify the essence of metaphysics. To such an attempt the restoration of metaphysics seems at first to be an overcoming, a conquest, which the exclusively metaphysical conception puts behind it in order to lead thinking into the open freedom of the restored essence of metaphysics. But in restoring, the enduring truth of the apparently rejected metaphysics now really returns to be henceforth its adopted *essence*.

Here something else takes place than a mere restoration of metaphysics. Besides, there is no restoration which could merely accept something handed down to it, as someone gathers the

Baum gefallenen Äpfel aufliest. Jede Restauration ist Interpretation der Metaphysik. Wer heute das metaphysische Fragen im Ganzen seiner Art und Geschichte deutlicher zu durchschauen und zu befolgen meint, sollte, wo er sich doch so überlegen gern in hellen Räumen bewegt, eines Tages darüber nachdenken, woher er denn das Licht zu einem klareren Sehen genommen hat. Das Groteske ist kaum mehr zu überbieten, daß man meine Denkversuche als Zertrümmerung der Metaphysik ausruft und sich gleichzeitig mit Hilfe jener Versuche auf Denkwegen und in Vorstellungen aufhält, die man jener angeblichen Zertrümmerung entnommen – ich sage nicht, zu verdanken – hat. Es braucht hier keinen Dank, aber eine Besinnung. Doch die Besinnungslosigkeit begann schon mit der oberflächlichen Mißdeutung der in »Sein und Zeit« (1927) erörterten »Destruktion«, die kein anderes Anliegen kennt, als im Abbau geläufig und leer gewordener Vorstellungen die ursprünglichen Seinserfahrungen der Metaphysik zurückzugewinnen.

Um jedoch die Metaphysik in ihrem Wesen zu retten, muß der Anteil der Sterblichen bei dieser Rettung sich darein bescheiden, erst einmal zu fragen: »Was ist Metaphysik?«. Auf die Gefahr, weitschweifig zu werden und anderwärts Gesagtes zu wiederholen, möchte ich die Gelegenheit dieses Briefes wahrnehmen, um den Sinn und die Tragweite jener Frage noch einmal zu erläutern. Weshalb? Weil auch *Ihr* Anliegen darauf geht, an der Überwindung des Nihilismus auf Ihre Weise mitzuhelfen. Solche Überwindung aber geschieht im Raume der Verwindung der Metaphysik. Diesen Raum betreten wir mit der Frage: »Was ist Metaphysik?« Die Frage enthält, nachdenklich gefragt, schon die Ahnung, daß ihre eigene Art zu fragen durch sie selbst ins Wanken gerät. »Was ist ...?« zeigt die Weise an, nach der man das »Wesen« zu erfragen pflegt. Wenn jedoch die Frage darauf geht, die Metaphysik als den Überstieg des Seins über das Seiende zu erörtern, dann wird mit dem übersteigenden »Sein« sogleich das Unterschiedene derjenigen Unterscheidung fragwürdig, worin sich von altersher die Lehren der Metaphysik bewegen, woher sie den Grundriß ihrer Sprache empfangen. Dies ist die Un-

apples which have dropped from the tree. Every restoration is an interpretation of metaphysics. Whoever believes that he can penetrate and follow metaphysical questions more clearly today in the entirety of their nature and history, should, since he likes to feel so superior as he moves in clear regions, consider one day whence he has taken the light to enable him to see more clearly. It is hardly possible to surpass the grotesqueness of proclaiming my attempts at thinking as smashing metaphysics to bits and of sojourning at the same time, with the help of those attempts, on paths of thinking and in conceptions which have been derived—I do not say, to which one is indebted—from that alleged demolition. There is no gratitude needed here, but some reflection. However, the lack of reflection already began with the superficial misinterpretation of the "destruction" which was discussed in *Sein und Zeit* (1927) and which has no other desire than to win back the original experiences of metaphysics as conceptions having become current and empty in the process of abandonment.

In order, nevertheless, to rescue metaphysics in its essence, the share of mortals in this rescue must be content with just asking first, "What is metaphysics?" At the risk of becoming tedious and of repeating what has been said elsewhere, I should like to take the opportunity afforded by this letter in order to explain once more the meaning and the importance of that question. Why? Because your desire is also aimed at helping in your way in the overcoming of nihilism. Such overcoming, however, takes place in the area of the restoration of metaphysics. We enter this area with the question, "What is metaphysics?" If thoughtfully asked, the question already contains the presentiment that its own way of putting the question begins to become shaky through itself. "What is . . .?" indicates the way in which one is accustomed to question the "essence." If, however, the question aims at discussing metaphysics as the transcendence of Being over being, then with the transcending "Being," that which has been differentiated in that differentiation, in which the tenets of metaphysics have moved since time immemorial and from which they obtain the basic outline of their language becomes subject to question. This is the

terscheidung von Wesen und Existenz, Was-sein und Daß-sein.

Die Frage: »Was ist Metaphysik?« macht zunächst arglos von dieser Unterscheidung Gebrauch. Alsbald erweist sich jedoch die Besinnung auf den Überstieg des Seins über das Seiende als eine jener Fragen, die sich selbst ins Herz stoßen müssen, nicht damit das Denken daran sterbe, sondern verwandelt lebe. Als ich die Frage: »Was ist Metaphysik?« zu erörtern versuchte – es geschah ein Jahr vor dem Erscheinen Ihrer Abhandlung »Die Totale Mobilmachung« –, strebte ich im voraus nicht nach einer Definition einer Disciplin der Schulphilosophie. Vielmehr erörterte ich im Hinblick auf die Bestimmung der Metaphysik, wonach in ihr der Überstieg über das Seiende als solches geschieht, eine Frage, die das Andere zum Seienden bedenkt. Aber auch diese Frage wurde nicht aus dem Ungefähren aufgegriffen und ins Unbestimmte hinaus gefragt.

Nach einem Vierteljahrhundert dürfte es an der Zeit sein, einmal auf eine Tatsache hinzuweisen, an der man auch heute noch vorbeigeht, gleich als sei es ein äußerlicher Umstand. Die Frage: »Was ist Metaphysik?« wurde in einer philosophischen Antrittsvorlesung vor allen versammelten Fakultäten erörtert. Sie stellt sich darum in den Kreis aller Wissenschaften und spricht zu diesen. Aber wie? Nicht in der anmaßlichen Absicht, deren Arbeit zu verbessern oder gar herabzusetzen.

Das Vorstellen der Wissenschaften geht überall auf das Seiende und zwar auf gesonderte Gebiete des Seienden. Es galt, von diesem Vorstellen des Seienden auszugehen und, ihm folgend, einer den Wissenschaften naheliegenden Meinung nachzugeben. Sie meinen, mit dem Vorstellen des Seienden sei der ganze Bezirk des Erforschbaren und Fragbaren erschöpft, außer dem Seienden gäbe es »sonst nichts«. Diese Meinung der Wissenschaften wird versuchsweise von der Frage nach dem Wesen der Metaphysik aufgenommen und dem Anschein nach mit ihnen geteilt. Indessen muß jeder Nachdenkende auch schon wissen, daß ein Fragen nach dem Wesen der Metaphysik einzig nur das im Blick haben kann, was die Meta-Physik auszeichnet: das ist der Überstieg: *das Sein des* Seienden. Im

differentiation between essence and existence, "to be—what" and "to be—so that."

The question, "What is metaphysics?" at first guilelessly makes use of this differentiation. Soon, however, there appears the consideration of the transcendence of Being over being as one of those questions which must stab themselves in the heart, not so that thinking should die from it but that it may live transformed. When I tried to discuss the question, "What is metaphysics?"—it occurred a year before the publication of your treatise *Total Mobilization*—I did not in advance strive for a definition of a discipline of school philosophy. Rather, in consideration of the determination of metaphysics, according to which the transcendence takes place over being as such, I discussed a question which considers the other side of being. But this question, too, was not picked up by mere chance and projected into vague and indefinite spaces.

After a quarter of a century the time may have come for once to point to a fact which is brushed aside even today, just as if it were an external circumstance. The question, "What is metaphysics?" was discussed at an opening philosophical lecture before the entire assembled faculties. It places itself, therefore, into the circle of all the sciences and speaks to them. But how? Not in the presumptuous intention of improving their work or, perhaps, of disparaging it.

The conception of the sciences is everywhere aimed at being and, indeed, at separated areas of being. It was necessary to start from this conception of being and, following it, to conform to an opinion close to the heart of the sciences. They believe that with the conception of being the entire field of what is explorable and subject to questioning has been exhausted, that except for being there is "nothing else." This opinion of the sciences is tentatively taken up with the question about the essence of metaphysics and apparently shared with them. However, every thoughtful person must already know that a questioning about the essence of metaphysics can only have in view what distinguishes metaphysics, and that is the transcendence: the *Being of* being.

Gesichtskreis des wissenschaftlichen Vorstellens, das nur das Seiende kennt, kann sich dagegen dasjenige, was ganz und gar kein Seiendes ist (nämlich das Sein), nur als Nichts darbieten. Darum frägt die Vorlesung nach »*diesem* Nichts«. Sie frägt nicht beliebig ins Unbestimmte nach «dem» Nichts. Sie frägt: wie steht es mit diesem ganz Anderen zu jeglichem Seienden, mit dem, was nicht ein Seiendes ist? Dabei zeigt sich: das Dasein des Menschen ist in »*dieses*« Nichts, in das ganz Andere zum Seienden, »hineingehalten«. Anders gewendet, heißt dies und konnte nur heißen: »Der Mensch ist der Platzhalter des Nichts.« Der Satz sagt: der Mensch hält dem ganz Anderen zum Seienden den Ort frei, sodaß es in dessen Offenheit dergleichen wie An-wesen (Sein) geben kann. Dieses Nichts, das nicht das Seiende ist und das *es* gleichwohl *gibt,* ist nichts Nichtiges. Es gehört zum An-wesen. Sein und Nichts gibt es nicht nebeneinander. Eines verwendet sich für das Andere in einer Verwandtschaft, deren Wesensfülle wir noch kaum bedacht haben. Wir bedenken sie auch nicht, solange wir zu fragen unterlassen: welches »Es« ist gemeint, das hier »gibt«? In welchem Geben gibt es? Inwiefern gehört zu diesem »Es gibt Sein und Nichts« solches, was sich dieser Gabe anheimgibt, indem es sie verwahrt? Leichthin sagen wir: es gibt. Das Sein »ist« so wenig wie das Nichts. Aber *Es gibt* beides.

Leonardo da Vinci schreibt: »Das Nichts hat keine Mitte, und seine Grenzen sind das Nichts.« – »Unter den großen Dingen, die unter uns zu finden sind, ist das Sein des Nichts das größte« (Tagebücher und Aufzeichnungen. Nach den italienischen Handschriften übersetzt und herausgegeben von Theodor Lücke 1940, S. 4 f.). Das Wort dieses Großen kann und soll nichts beweisen; aber es weist in die Fragen: Auf welche Art gibt es Sein, gibt es Nichts? Woher kommt uns solches Geben? Inwiefern sind wir schon an es vergeben, sofern wir als Menschenwesen sind?

Weil die Vorlesung »Was ist Metaphysik?« gemäß der ergriffenen Gelegenheit mit absichtlicher Beschränkung aus dem Hinblick auf den Überstieg, d. h. auf das *Sein des* Seienden, nach *jenem* Nichts frägt, das sich zunächst für das wissenschaftliche Vorstellen des Seienden ergibt, hat man aus dem

Within the horizon of scientific conception, which only knows being, that which is not being (namely Being) in any way at all can, on the other hand, present itself only as nothingness. Therefore, the lecture asks about *"this* nothingness." It does not ask haphazardly and vaguely about "the" nothingness. It asks: how about this totally different other to each being, that which is not being? In this it is shown that man's existence is "held into" *"this"* nothingness, into this completely other of being. Put differently, this means, and could only mean, "Man is the seat-holder for nothingness." This sentence means that man is holding the place open for the complete other of being, so that in its openness there can be such a thing as being present (Being). This nothingness which is not being but *is* just the same, is nothing negative. It belongs to being present. Being and nothingness are not side by side. One intercedes on behalf of the other in a relationship, the amplitude of whose essence we have scarcely considered yet. Nor do we consider it as long as we refrain from asking which "it" is meant that "is" [giving] here. In what kind of giving does it give? In what respect does there belong to this "there is Being and nothingness" such a thing which submits to this gift of existence while preserving it? Lightly we say: there is. Being "is" just as little as nothingness, but both *are*.

Leonardo de Vinci writes: "Nothingness has no middle, and its boundaries are nothingness."—"Among the great things which are to be found among us, the Being of nothingness is the greatest." (*Diaries and Notes.* Translated from the Italian manuscripts and edited by Theodore Lücke, 1940, p. 4f.) The words of this great man cannot and are not supposed to prove anything; but they point to the questions: In which way is Being [given], is nothingness [given]? Whence does such giving arise? In which respect are we given up to it, in so far as we are the essence of man?

Because, in view of the opportunity at hand, the lecture *What is Metaphysics?* asks with intentional limitation out of the consideration for transcendence, that is, the *Being of* being asks about *that* nothingness which first arises for the scientific conception of being, *the* nothingness was picked out of the lecture

Vortrag »das« Nichts aufgegriffen und ihn zu einem Dokument des Nihilismus gemacht. Nach geraumer Zeit dürfte jetzt einmal die Frage erlaubt sein: wo, in welchem Satz und in welcher Wendung ist jemals gesagt, das in der Vorlesung genannte Nichts sei das Nichts im Sinne des nichtigen Nichts und als dieses das erste und letzte Ziel alles Vorstellens und Existierens?

Die Vorlesung schließt mit der Frage: »Warum ist überhaupt Seiendes und nicht vielmehr Nichts?«. Hier ist mit Absicht und gegen die Gewohnheit »Nichts« groß geschrieben? Nach dem Wortlaut allerdings wird hier die Frage vorgebracht, die Leibniz gestellt und Schelling aufgenommen hat. Beide Denker verstehen sie als die Frage nach dem obersten Grund und der ersten seienden Ursache für alles Seiende. Die heutigen Versuche, die Metaphysik zu restaurieren, nehmen die gekennzeichnete Frage mit Vorliebe auf.

Aber die Vorlesung »Was ist Metaphysik?« denkt gemäß ihrem andersgearteten Weg durch einen anderen Bereich auch diese Frage in einem verwandelten Sinne. Gefragt ist jetzt: woran liegt es, daß überall nur das Seiende den Vorrang hat, daß nicht eher das Nicht des Seienden, »dieses Nichts«, d. h. das Sein hinsichtlich seines Wesens bedacht wird? Wer die Vorlesung als eine Strecke des Weges von »Sein und Zeit« durchdenkt, kann die Frage nur in dem erwähnten Sinne verstehen. Dies zu versuchen, war zunächst eine befremdliche Zumutung. Darum wurde die gewandelte Frage ausdrücklich in der »Einleitung« erläutert (S. 20 ff.), die der fünften Auflage von »Was ist Metaphysik?« (1949) vorangestellt ist.

Was soll dieser Hinweis? Er soll andeuten, wie schwerfällig und zögernd sich das Denken auf eine Besinnung einläßt, die dem nachsinnt, was auch das Anliegen Ihrer Schrift »Über die Linie« bleibt: das Wesen des Nihilismus.

Die Frage: »Was ist Metaphysik?« versucht nur das eine: die Wissenschaften zum Nachdenken darüber zu bringen, daß sie notwendig und darum jederzeit und überall auf das ganz Andere zum Seienden, auf das Nichts an Seiendem treffen. Sie stehen ohne *ihr* Wissen schon im Bezug zum Sein. Sie empfangen nur aus der jeweils waltenden Wahrheit des Seins ein

and it was turned into a document of nihilism. After ample time has elapsed the question might now be permitted: where, in which sentence and in which turn of a phrase is it ever said that the nothingness named in the lecture is nothingness in the sense of negated nothingness and as such is the first and last goal of all conception and existence?

The lecture closes with the question: "Why is there being at all and not rather Nothingness? Here "Nothingness" is intentionally and, contrary to previous procedure, written with a capital. According to the wording the question is, to be sure, broached which Leibniz posed and Schelling took up. Both thinkers understand it as the question about the highest reason and the first existing cause for all being. Present-day attempts to restore metaphysics have a special liking for taking up the designated question.

But the lecture *What is Metaphysics?* in accordance with its differently constituted way through another area, also thinks this question in a transformed sense. It is now asked: what is the reason why everywhere being is given precedence, why the negative of being, "this nothingness," that is, Being in regard to its essence, is not rather considered? Whoever thinks through the lecture as a stretch of the road from *Sein und Zeit* can understand the question only in the sense mentioned. To attempt this was at first a strange and exacting demand. That is why the transformed question was expressly explained in the "Introduction" (pp. 20ff.), which precedes the fifth edition of *What is Metaphysics* (1949).

What is the reference meant to do? It is supposed to indicate how slowly and haltingly thinking enters into a consideration which reflects on that which is also the concern of your article *Across the Line,* the essence of nihilism.

The question, "What is metaphysics?" only attempts the one thing: to induce the sciences to reflect that they necessarily, and, for that reason, always and everywhere encounter the complete other of being, the nothingness belonging to being. Even without *their* knowledge they are already in relation to Being. They receive only from the occasionally prevailing truth of Be-

Licht, um das von ihnen vorgestellte Seiende *als ein solches* erst sehen und betrachten zu können. Das Fragen »Was ist Metaphysik?«, d. h. das aus ihr herkommende Denken ist nicht mehr Wissenschaft. Für das Denken aber wird nun der Überstieg als solcher, d. h. *das Sein des* Seienden hinsichtlich seines Wesens fragwürdig und darum niemals nichtswürdig und nichtig. Das anscheinend leere Wort »Sein« ist dabei stets in der Wesensfülle derjenigen Bestimmungen gedacht, die von der *Φύσις* und dem *Λόγος* her bis zum »Willen zur Macht« aufeinander verweisen und überall einen Grundzug zeigen, der im Wort »An-wesen« (Sein und Zeit, § 6) zu nennen versucht wird. Nur *weil* die Frage: »Was ist Metaphysik?« im vorhinein an den Überstieg, an das transcendens, an das *Sein des* Seienden denkt, kann sie das Nicht des Seienden, *jenes* Nichts denken, das gleichursprünglich das Selbe ist mit dem Sein.

Wer nun freilich die Grundrichtung der Frage nach der Metaphysik, den Ausgang ihres Weges, die Gelegenheit ihrer Entfaltung, den Kreis der Wissenschaften, zu denen sie gesprochen ist, nie ernstlich und im Zusammenhang bedacht hat, muß auf die Auskunft verfallen, hier werde eine Philosophie des Nichts (im Sinne des negativen Nihilismus) vorgetragen.

Die anscheinend noch nicht ausrottbaren Mißdeutungen der Frage: »Was ist Metaphysik?« und das Verkennen ihres Standortes sind zum geringsten Teil nur Folgen einer Abneigung gegen das Denken. Ihr Ursprung liegt tiefer verborgen. Sie gehören indes zu den Erscheinungen, die unseren Geschichtsgang beleuchten: wir bewegen uns mit dem ganzen Bestand noch innerhalb der Zone des Nihilismus, gesetzt freilich, das Wesen des Nihilismus beruhe in der Seinsvergessenheit.

Wie steht es dann mit dem Überqueren der Linie? Führt es aus der Zone des vollendeten Nihilismus heraus? Der Versuch des Überquerens der Linie bleibt in ein Vorstellen gebannt, das in den Herrschaftsbereich der Seinsvergessenheit gehört. Darum spricht es auch in den metaphysischen Grundbegriffen (Gestalt, Wert, Transzendenz).

Kann das Bild der Linie die Zone des vollendeten Nihilismus zureichend veranschaulichen? Steht es mit dem Bild der Zone besser?

ing a light in order to be able first to see and observe *as such* the being conceived by them. The questioning as to what metaphysics, that is, the thinking coming from it, is, is no longer science. For thinking, however, transcendence as such, that is, *the Being of* being now becomes worthy of question in regard to its essence and therefore never worthless and negative. The apparently empty word "Being" is always thought of in the amplitude of the essence of those determinations which, beginning with the *thusis* and the *Logos,* point the way one after the other up to the "will to power" and everywhere show a basic characteristic which the word "being present" (*Sein und Zeit,* § 6) has attempted to designate. Only because the question, "What is metaphysics?" thinks from the beginning of the climbing above, the transcendence, the *Being of* being, can it think of the negative of being, of *that* nothingness which just as originally is identical with Being.

Now, to be sure, whoever has never seriously considered the basic direction of the question about metaphysics, the outcome of its path, the occasion of its unfolding, and the circle of the sciences to which it is addressed, and has never considered it in association with all of these, must resort to the information that a philosophy of nothingness (in the sense of negative nihilism) is presented here.

The misinterpretation of the question, "What is metaphysics?" which apparently can not yet be stamped out, and the failure to recognize its stopping-place are to the smallest extent only consequences of an aversion to thinking. Their origin lies more deeply hidden. They belong, however, to the pheonomena which illuminate the course of our history: we are still moving with all of our component realities within the zone of nihilism, assuming, to be sure, that the essence of nihilism is based on the oblivion of Being.

How about the crossing of the line? Does it lead out of the zone of complete nihilism? The attempt to cross the line remains inhibited in a conception which belongs in the area of dominance of the oblivion of Being. That is why it also speaks in the basic metaphysical concepts (*Gestalt,* value, transcendence).

Can the image of the line furnish an adequate illustration for the zone of complete nihilism? Is the image of the zone better?

Zweifel regen sich, ob solche Bilder geeignet sind, die Überwindung des Nihilismus, d. h. die Verwindung der Seinsvergessenheit zu veranschaulichen. Doch vermutlich unterliegt jedes Bild solchen Zweifeln. Gleichwohl vermögen sie die erleuchtende Kraft der Bilder, ihre ursprüngliche und unumgehbare Gegenwart nicht anzutasten. Überlegungen solcher Art bezeugen nur, wie wenig wir in der Sage des Denkens bewandert sind und ihr Wesen kennen.

Das Wesen des Nihilismus, der sich zuletzt in die Herrschaft des Willens zum Willen vollendet, beruht in der Seinsvergessenheit. Ihr scheinen wir am ehesten zu entsprechen, wenn wir sie vergessen und d. h. hier: in den Wind schlagen. Aber so achten wir nicht auf das, was Vergessenheit als Verborgenheit des S̶e̶i̶n̶s̶ besagt. Achten wir darauf, dann erfahren wir die bestürzende Notwendigkeit: statt den Nihilismus überwinden zu wollen, müssen wir versuchen, erst in sein *Wesen* einzukehren. Die Einkehr in sein Wesen ist der erste Schritt, durch den wir den Nihilismus hinter uns lassen. Der Weg dieser Einkehr hat die Richtung und Art einer Rückkehr. Sie meint freilich nicht ein Rückwärts zu abgelebten Zeiten, um diese versuchsweise in einer gekünstelten Form aufzufrischen. Das Zurück nennt hier die Richtung auf jene Ortschaft (die Seinsvergessenheit), aus der schon die Metaphysik ihre Herkunft empfing und behält.

Dieser Herkunft gemäß bleibt es der Metaphysik verwehrt, als Metaphysik jemals ihr Wesen zu erfahren; denn für den Überstieg und innerhalb seiner *zeigt* sich dem metaphysischen Vorstellen das *Sein* des Seienden. Auf solche Weise erscheinend, nimmt es das metaphysische Vorstellen eigens in den Anspruch. Kein Wunder, daß sich dieses gegen den Gedanken auflehnt, es bewege sich in der Seins*vergessenheit*.

Und dennoch gewinnt eine zureichende und ausdauernde Besinnung den Einblick: die Metaphysik verstattet ihrem Wesen nach dem menschlichen Wohnen nie, sich eigens in der Ortschaft, d. h. im Wesen der Seinsvergessenheit anzusiedeln. Darum muß das Denken und Dichten dorthin zurück, wo es in gewisser Weise immer schon gewesen ist und gleichwohl noch nie baute. Wir können jedoch nur durch ein Bauen das Wohnen in jener Ortschaft bereiten. Solches Bauen darf kaum schon auf

Doubts are stirring whether such images are suited to illustrate the overcoming of nihilism, that is, the restoration of the oblivion of Being. However, presumably every image is subject to such doubts. Nevertheless, they are not able to touch the illuminating force of the images and their original and unavoidable presence. Such considerations only show how slight is our acquaintance with the language of thinking and our knowledge of its essence.

The essence of nihilism which finally is fulfilled in the dominance of the will to will, is based on the oblivion of Being. We seem to be related to it most easily when we forget it, and that means here, disregard it. But in so doing we do not pay attention to what oblivion as concealment of ~~Being~~ means. If we pay attention to it, then we experience the dismaying necessity that instead of wanting to overcome nihilism we must try first to enter into its *essence*. The entry into its essence is the first step by which we leave nihilism behind us. The path of this entry has the direction and manner of a going back. It does not, to be sure, mean a going backward to times lived through in the past in order to refresh them tentatively in an artificial form. The "back" here designates the direction towards that locality (the oblivion of Being), from out of which metaphysics obtained and retains its origin.

In accordance with this origin, metaphysics is prevented from ever learning its essence as metaphysics because, for the transcendence, and within it, the *Being* of being *shows* itself to metaphysical conception. Appearing in such a fashion, it expressly lays claim to metaphysical conception. No wonder that the latter rebels against the thought that it is moving in the *oblivion* of Being.

And yet an adequate and persevering reflection succeeds in seeing that metaphysics never permits its essence after a human dwelling to settle purposely in the locality, that is, in the essence of the oblivion of Being. For that reason, thinking and speculation must return to where they have in a certain way always been and yet have never built. We can, however, only prepare for dwelling in a locality by building. Such building may scarcely

die Errichtung des Hauses für den Gott und der Wohnstätten für die Sterblichen sinnen. Es muß sich begnügen, am *Weg* zu bauen, der in die Ortschaft der Verwindung der Metaphysik zurückführt und dadurch das Geschickliche einer Überwindung des Nihilismus durchwandern läßt.

Wer ein solches Wort wagt und gar in öffentlicher Schrift, weiß zu gut, wie übereilt und leicht dieses Sagen, das eine Besinnung veranlassen möchte, nur als dunkles Raunen abgestellt oder als herrisches Verkünden zurückgewiesen wird. Dessen ungeachtet muß der immerfort Lernende darauf denken, die Sage des andenkenden Denkens ursprünglicher und sorgsamer zu prüfen. Eines Tages gelangt er dahin, dieses Sagen als höchstes Geschenk und größte Gefahr, als selten Geglücktes und oft Mißglücktes im Geheimnisvollen zu lassen.

Hier erkennen wir, weshalb jedes Sagen dieser Art sich im Unbeholfenen weitermüht. Immer geht es durch die wesenhafte Mehrdeutigkeit des Wortes und seiner Wendungen hindurch. Die Mehrdeutigkeit der Sage besteht keineswegs in einer bloßen Anhäufung beliebig auftauchender Bedeutungen. Sie beruht in einem Spiel, das, je reicher es sich entfaltet, um so strenger in einer verborgenen Regel gehalten bleibt. Durch diese spielt die Mehrdeutigkeit im Ausgewogenen, dessen Schwingung wir selten erfahren. Darum bleibt die Sage ins höchste Gesetz gebunden. Das ist die Freiheit, die in das allspielende Gefüge der nie ruhenden Verwandlung befreit. Die Mehrdeutigkeit jener Worte, die »wie Blumen entstehen« (Hölderlin, Brod und Wein), ist der Garten der Wildnis, worin Wachstum und Pflege aus einer unbegreiflichen Innigkeit zueinander gestimmt sind. Es dürfte Sie nicht verwundern, daß die Erörterung des Wesens des Nihilismus unausweichlich an jeder Wegstelle auf das erregend Denkwürdige trifft, das wir unbeholfen genug die Sage des Denkens nennen. Diese Sage ist nicht der Ausdruck des Denkens, sondern es selber, sein Gang und Sang.

Was möchte dieser Brief? Er versucht, die Überschrift »Über die Linie«, d. h. alles, was sie in Ihrem und in meinem Sinne beschriftet und im schreibenden Sagen zu erweisen verstattet, in eine höhere Mehrdeutigkeit zu heben. Diese läßt erfahren,

have in mind the erection of the house for God and of the dwelling places for mortals. It must be content with constructing the *road* which leads into the locality of the restoration of metaphysics and thereby permits a walk through the destined phase of an overcoming of nihilism.

Whoever dares to say such things and what is more, in writing which is open to the public, knows only too well how prematurely and easily these words, which would only like to induce some reflection, are only shut off as murky rumblings or are rejected as arbitrary pronouncements. Regardless of this, he who is continually learning must think of testing the language of reflective thinking in a more original and more careful manner. One day he will reach the point of leaving in the realm of the mysterious this language as the highest gift and the greatest danger, as something rarely successful and often unsuccessful.

Here we recognize why every form of expression of this sort struggles on in awkwardness. It always goes through the essential meaning-fullness of words and phraseology. The meaning-fullness of language by no means consists in a mere accumulation of meanings cropping up haphazardly. It is based on a play which, the more richly it unfolds, the more strictly it is bound by a hidden rule. Through this, meaning-fullness plays a part in what has been selected and weighed in the scale whose oscillations we seldom experience. That is why what is said is bound by the highest law. That is the freedom which gives freedom to the all-playing structure of never-resting transformation. The meaning-fullness of those words, which "originate like flowers" (Hölderlin, *Bread and Wine*), is the garden of the jungle, in which growth and cultivation harmonize with one another out of an incomprehensible intimacy. You should not be surprised that the discussion of the essence of nihilism unavoidably encounters at every point in the road something worthy of stimulating thinking which we awkwardly enough call the language of thinking. This language is not the expression of thinking, but is thinking itself, its stride and its voice.

What would this letter like to do? It is trying to lift into a higher meaning-fullness the title *Across the Line*, that is, everything which it writes about in your and in my sense and tries to say in written form. This meaning-fullness lets it be known

inwiefern die Überwindung des Nihilismus die Einkehr in dessen Wesen verlangt, mit welcher Einkehr das Überwindenwollen hinfällig wird. Die Verwindung der Metaphysik ruft das Denken in ein anfänglicheres Geheiß.

Ihre Lagebeurteilung trans lineam und meine Erörterung de linea sind aufeinander angewiesen. Zusammen bleiben sie dahin verwiesen, nicht von der Bemühung abzulassen, auf einer Strecke Weges, und sei sie noch so kurz bemessen, das planetarische Denken einzuüben. Es bedarf auch hier keiner prophetischen Gaben und Gebärden, um daran zu denken, daß dem planetarischen Bauen Begegnungen bevorstehen, denen die Begegnenden heute auf keiner Seite gewachsen sind. Dies gilt für die europäische Sprache und für die ostasiatische in gleicher Weise, gilt vor alldem für den Bereich ihrer möglichen Zwiesprache. Keine von beiden vermag von sich aus diesen Bereich zu öffnen und zu stiften.

Nietzsche, in dessen Licht und Schatten jeder Heutige mit seinem »für ihn« oder »wider ihn« denkt und dichtet, hörte ein Geheiß, das eine Vorbereitung des Menschen für die Übernahme einer Erdherrschaft verlangt. Er sah und verstand den entbrennenden Kampf um die Herrschaft (XIV, S. 320, XVI, S. 337, XII, S. 208). Es ist kein Krieg, sondern der $\Pi\acute{o}\lambda\epsilon\mu o\varsigma$, der Götter und Menschen, Freie und Knechte erst in ihr jeweiliges Wesen erscheinen läßt und eine Aus-einander-setzung des Seins heraufführt. Mit ihr verglichen, bleiben Weltkriege vordergründig. Sie vermögen immer weniger zu entscheiden, je technischer sie sich rüsten.

Nietzsche hörte jenes Geheiß zur Besinnung auf das Wesen einer planetarischen Herrschaft. Er folgte dem Ruf auf dem Weg des ihm beschiedenen metaphysischen Denkens und stürzte unterwegs. So erscheint es wenigstens der historischen Betrachtung. Vielleicht aber stürzte er nicht, sondern gelangte so weit, wie sein Denken es konnte.

Daß es Schweres und Schwieriges zurückließ, sollte uns strenger und anders noch als bisher daran erinnern, aus welch langer Herkunft die in ihm erwachte Frage nach dem Wesen des Nihilismus stammt. Die Frage ist für uns nicht leichter geworden. Darum muß sie sich auf Vorläufigeres einschränken:

in which way the overcoming of nihilism demands an entry into its essence, with which entry the desire to overcome breaks down. The restoration of metaphysics calls thinking into a more primordial demand.

Your *trans lineam* estimation of the situation and my discussion *de linea* are dependent upon one another. Together they are obliged not to give up the effort to practice planetary thinking along a stretch of the road, be it ever so short. Here too no prophetic talents and demeanor are needed to realize that there are in store for planetary building encounters to which participants are by no means equal today. This is equally true of the European and of the East Asiatic languages and, above all, for the area of a possible conversation between them. Neither of the two is able by itself to open up this area and to establish it.

Nietzsche, in whose light and shadow everyone today thinks and reflects with his "for him" or "against him," heard a command which demands a preparation of man for taking over a world-domination. He saw and understood the conflict for domination about to be enkindled (XIV, p. 320; XVI, p. 337; XII, p. 208). This is not a war, but the *Polemos,* which causes gods and men, free men and serfs first to appear in their essence and brings about a setting-apart of ~~Being~~. Compared with it, World Wars remain in the foreground. They are able to decide less and less the more technological their armament becomes.

Nietzsche heard that command to reflect on the essence of a planetary domination. He followed the call along the path of the metaphysical thinking with which he was endowed and he broke down on the way. So it seems, at least, to historical observation. Perhaps he did not collapse, however, but on the contrary, went as far as his thinking permitted.

That it left behind weighty and difficult matters, should remind us more strongly, and in a different way from before, from what a distant past stems the question which awakened in him as to the essence of nihilism. The question has not become any easier for us. For that reason, it must restrict itself

alten, ehrwürdigen Worten nachdenken, deren Sage uns den Wesensbereich des Nihilismus und seiner Verwindung zuspricht. Gibt es eine bemühtere Rettung des uns Geschickten und im Geschick Überlieferten als solches Andenken? Ich wüßte keine. Aber es erscheint denen als umstürzend, für die das Herkömmliche ohne Herkunft bleibt. Das arglos Scheinende nehmen sie auch schon für das absolut Gültige. Sie fordern, daß dies in großaufgemachten Systemen erscheine. Wo hingegen das Nachdenken sich immer nur damit abgibt, auf den Sprachgebrauch des Denkens aufmerksam zu machen, bringt es keinen Nutzen. Aber zuweilen dient es dem, was das zu-Denkende braucht.

Was der Brief darzulegen versucht, mag sich allzubald als unzulänglich erweisen.

Wie er jedoch Besinnung und Erörterung pflegen möchte, sagt Goethe in einem Satz, der diesen Brief beschließen möge:

»Wenn jemand Wort und Ausdruck als heilige Zeugnisse betrachtet und sie nicht etwa, wie Scheidemünze oder Papiergeld, nur zu schnellem, augenblicklichem Verkehr bringen, sondern im geistigen Handel und Wandel als wahres Äquivalent ausgetauscht wissen will, so kann man ihm nicht verübeln, daß er aufmerksam macht, wie herkömmliche Ausdrücke, woran niemand mehr Arges hat, doch einen schädlichen Einfluß verüben, Ansichten verdüstern, den Begriff entstellen und ganzen Fächern eine falsche Richtung geben.«

Ich grüße Sie herzlich.

to something more temporary: to reflect on old, venerable words the language of which gives us promise of the realm of the essence of nihilism and of its restoration. Is there a rescue of what is destined for us and of what has been handed down to us by destiny more worthy of effort than such reflection? None that I know of. But it seems revolutionary to those who do not ask whence comes what has come down to us. They regard what seems to look innocent as already absolutely valid. They demand that it appear in elaborate systems. When, on the other hand, reflection is always concerned only with drawing attention to the use thinking makes of language, this is of no value. But at times it does serve that which needs the thinking process.

What this letter is trying to demonstrate may prove all too soon to be inadequate.

How it would like, however, to cultivate reflection and discussion, Goethe says in the statement with which I should like to close this letter:

"If anyone regards words and expressions as sacred testimonials and does not put them, like currency and paper money, into quick and immediate circulation, but wants to see them exchanged in the intellectual trade and barter as true equivalents, then one can not blame him if he draws attention to the fact that traditional expressions, at which no one any longer takes offense, nevertheless exert a damaging influence, confuse opinions, distort understanding, and give entire fields of subject-matter a false direction."

I send you my hearty greetings.